1001
horrible
FACTS

A yukkopedia of gross
truths about everything...

Anne Rooney

ARCTURUS

ARCTURUS

Arcturus Publishing Limited
26/27 Bickels Yard
151–153 Bermondsey Street
London SE1 3HA

Published in association with
foulsham
W. Foulsham & Co. Ltd,
The Publishing House, Bennetts Close, Cippenham,
Slough, Berkshire SL1 5AP, England

ISBN: 978-0-572 03446-7

This edition printed in 2008
Copyright © 2006 Arcturus Publishing Limited

British Library Cataloguing-in-Publication Data: a catalogue
record for this book is available from the British Library

Printed in Singapore

Design and Illustration by ℚ CREATIVE QUOTIENT

Author: Anne Rooney
The right of Anne Rooney to be identified as the author of this work
has been asserted under the Copyright, Designs and Patent Act, 1988.
The author can be contacted at anne@annerooney.co.uk

Goblin cover illustration by Steve Beaumont

Editor: Rebecca Gerlings

CONTENTS

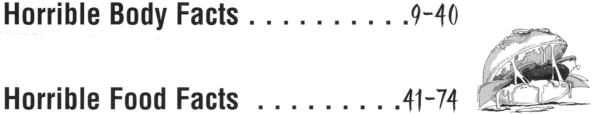

1001 horrible Facts

PASS THE BUCKET...

Even if you can boast a gross little brother or sister who picks their nose or farts in your sleeping bag, believe it or not there are things going on right now all over the world that are far, far yukkier than that. Fully grown adults who should know better do some really horrible things, too.

For instance, did you know that in some places people don't let their dead rest in peace, keeping them up all hours (and years) joining in family celebrations? Or that in other places people eat rotten food – and not because they forgot to go to the shops, but because they actually *like* it? Did you know that some animals eat their dinner while it's still alive? And do you know what's living in your body – apart from you? Would you like to find out? Then this is the book for you!

Try to have a bucket handy – or you could pick up some sickness bags next time you go on a ship or a plane.

Air sickness bag facts:

(Free extras, not part of your 1001 facts!)

Virgin Atlantic got top designers to work on its air sickness bags. The cost of a full set of 20 stylish bags has been known to reach triple figures.

You can buy rare air sickness bags on ebay.

The world's largest collection of air sickness bags is owned by Niek Vermeulen of the Netherlands who has 3,728 of them, from 802 airlines.

A British Airways air sickness bag from 1996 has instructions (for what? – vomiting?) in 11 languages – which is a record, apparently.

There is an email group for people who want to swap (unused) air sickness bags.

Your turn

If there was such a thing as the University of Yuk, you'd graduate from it with flying colours by the time you reach the end of this book. That's why you'll be more than qualified to fill in your own yukkiest fact on the very last page to complete the grand total of 1001. Perhaps you know a really yukky fact that we've missed? Or has something really gross happened to you? Was your cat sick on your snack? (And did you notice before you ate it?) Or did the book make *you* sick on your snack? Whatever your yukkiest fact might be, you know what to do.

Now, ready to cringe? Then read on...

Don't try this at home!

There are some pretty yukky things in this book
— in fact, some are world records in grossness.
But that doesn't mean you should try to out-
gross them yourself. Some are really rather
dangerous, and people have spent years training
themselves to do them. Can you *imagine*
training for years to hang from your ear-lobes
or gobble snails? Why would you? Get a life!
More importantly, keep the life you've got!
If you happen to find yourself burping non-stop
for 90 years or growing an eyebrow as long as a
battleship, get in touch with the *Guinness Book of
World Records*. Otherwise, leave it to the experts.

Horrible Body Facts

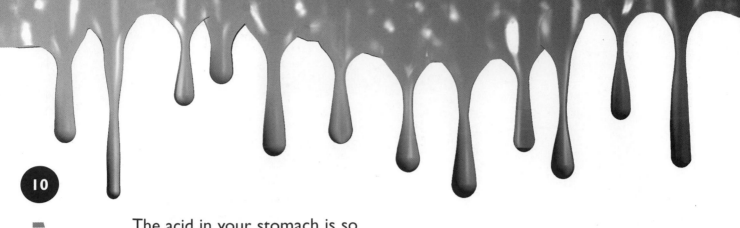

The acid in your stomach is so strong that it can dissolve steel razor blades – it's still not a good idea to eat them, though!

Anne Boleyn, one of King Henry VIII's six wives, had six fingers on each hand and an extra nipple. This was claimed to be evidence of witchcraft and was used in her trial when Henry had her executed in 1536.

More than 100 million micro-organisms live in your mouth at any time.

A beef tapeworm, caught from eating eggs in infected beef, can grow to 12 metres (39 feet) long in the human gut.

Egyptian mummies that have been dead for 3,000 years still have their fingerprints intact.

In the old days, children being trained as acrobats for circuses were strapped into strange and often very painful positions to make their bodies more bendy.

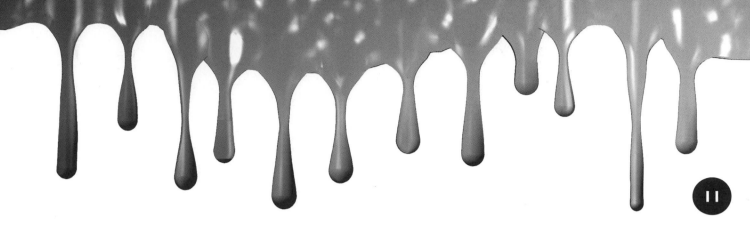

In 1970, a thief was caught in Zurich, Switzerland, when a finger that had been cut off by broken glass at the crime scene was matched to his finger prints in police records.

Girls who made matches in the 1800s often suffered from 'phossy jaw' – their jaw bones would rot away, poisoned by the phosphorus used to make the matches.

The average person loses 200 millilitres (7 fluid ounces) of water a day in their faeces.

The maw-worm can grow to 30 centimetres (1 foot) and then come out of the body from any gap or hole, including the corner of the eye.

You go white when really scared because blood drains from your skin. This protected primitive humans from bleeding to death if bitten by scary, wild animals.

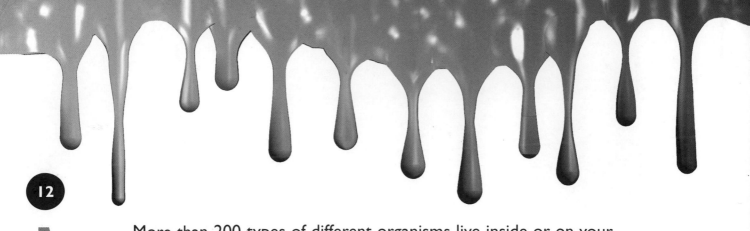

More than 200 types of different organisms live inside or on your body at any time.

In 1973, Italian kidnappers were paid a ransom of over $3 million after they cut off the ear of their kidnap victim and sent it to his very rich grandfather, John Paul Getty.

If you could scrunch together all the bacteria living on the outside of your body, they would take up about the same amount of space as one pea.

All the bacteria living inside your body would fill six teaspoons.

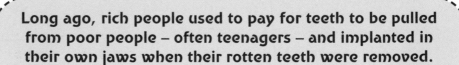

Long ago, rich people used to pay for teeth to be pulled from poor people – often teenagers – and implanted in their own jaws when their rotten teeth were removed.

If your vomit looks like what you've just eaten, that's exactly what it is. If it's soupy, then it's because it's been in your stomach for a while.

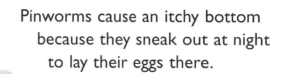

Pinworms cause an itchy bottom because they sneak out at night to lay their eggs there.

Ten billion scales of skin fall off your body every day.

When diarrhoea turns pale, it contains bits of the lining of your gut.

Urine doesn't contain bacteria. Becalmed or shipwrecked sailors used to drink it with no ill-effects.

Dentists in the Far East used to pull teeth out with their bare hands! In China, they practised by pulling nails out of wood with their fingers.

Your body needs sleep. Staying awake for two weeks can be enough to kill you.

Adult feet produce about a quarter of a cup of sweat a day from 250,000 pores – wait four days and you could make a cup of foot-sweat tea!

Foods that will make you fart include beans, bran, broccoli, sprouts, cabbage, cauliflower and onions.

The larvae of the pork tapeworm, hatched from eggs eaten in infected pork, can travel around the body and live in the brain, eyes, heart or muscles.

At least 1.3 billion people are infected with a small hookworm that attaches to the inside of the gut. If there are a lot, it looks like fur or a thick carpet. Around the world, they suck a total of 10 million litres (around 21 million pints) of blood a day.

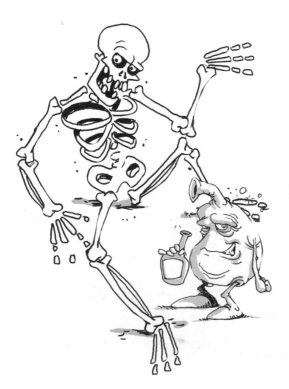

An Indian man known as Snake Manu can put small snakes, including deadly cobras, into his mouth and pass them out through his nose.

In Ancient Mexico, people bound their babies' heads tightly to make their skulls long and thin.

Surma girls of Ethiopia put clay disks in their lower lip, stretching the lip outwards. The size of the disk indicates how many cattle a man needs to provide to marry the girl – they can be up to 15 centimetres (6 inches) across.

When a wound gets infected, it oozes yellow pus. Pus is a mixture of dead blood cells, bacteria and other dead cells from your body.

Prickly heat rash is caused by sweat sticking to the layer of dead skin cells on top of your skin. As the cells can't fall off, the sweat can't escape and makes the live cells underneath swell up.

Most people have mites – very tiny creatures related to spiders – living in their eyelashes, eyebrows, ears and noses.

For a work entitled *Self*, created in 1991, English sculptor Marc Quinn made a copy of his head, moulded from his own deep-frozen blood. Quinn collected almost 4 litres (8 pints) of his blood over five months, poured it into a mould of his head and froze it.

About 70 millilitres (around 2.5 fluid ounces) of blood are spurted out of your heart with each beat.

The wucheria worm can live in the lymph system and grow up to 12 centimetres (5 inches) long.

About a third of your faeces is not old food, but bacteria that help you to digest food, and bits of the lining of the inside of your gut.

In some countries, the umbilical cord – the cord that attaches the unborn baby to its mother – is dried and kept after birth, to use in spells or medicines.

In some parts of Africa and on some Pacific islands, people make patterns of raised scars on their skin as a decoration or to show their bravery. The wounds are made with sharp spikes or thorns from plants and often rubbed with special kinds of earth or leaves to created coloured tattoos.

Pilgrims to the Tirupati temple in India give some of their hair as a sacrifice. The temple employs 600 barbers who work day and night to shave pilgrims, taking 6.5 million gifts of hair a year. The hair is sold to wig-makers and for use as fertilizer.

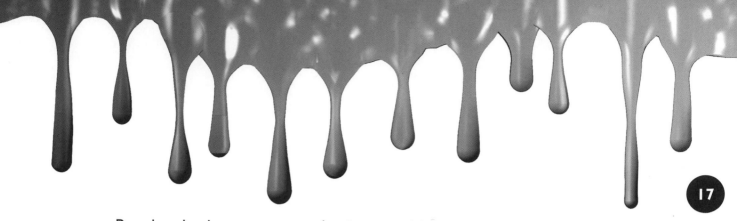

People who lose an arm or leg in an accident or operation can often still feel it hurting, aching or itching but can do nothing to make it feel better.

Dust mites are found in all houses. They eat the dead skin we shed all the time, and live in beds, carpets, rugs and anywhere else snug which collects flakes of skin.

If you unravelled all the tiny tubes in your kidneys and laid them end to end, they would stretch 80 kilometres (50 miles). Yet they scrunch up to fit into kidneys only 10 centimetres (4 inches) long.

An amoeba common in warm water can travel up your nose while you are swimming and live in your brain, where it multiplies rapidly and kills you in three to seven days.

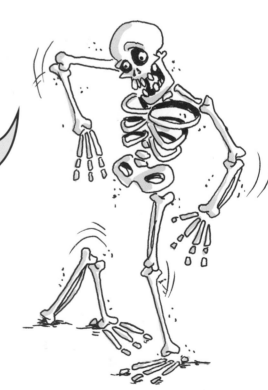

You will produce 45,000 litres (around 95,000 pints) of urine in your life – enough to fill a small swimming pool!

The old Chinese medical technique of acupuncture involves sticking lots of very thin needles into a person's body. The theory is that putting the needles on 'energy pathways' around the body relieves pain and cures illness.

Head lice can change colour to merge in with the hair they are hiding in.

Urine is a good remedy for jellyfish stings, so if you're standing in the sea and get stung, just urinate down your legs.

Liposuction is a popular operation in Europe and the USA amongst people who feel they are too fat. A surgeon sticks a long, hollow needle into the fat part – such as the tummy or thighs – uses ultrasound to turn the fat to yellow mush, and then sucks it out through the needle.

Athlete's foot is a fungus that grows in the warm, sweaty spaces between your toes. It causes itching and split skin.

The palms of the hands are the sweatiest parts of the body, followed by the feet.

When Ancient Egyptians mummified someone, they used a special long-handled spoon to scoop the brains out through the dead person's nose. They often fed the brain to animals.

The medical name for ear wax is *cerumen*; it is produced by more than 4,000 glands in your ears.

If you don't brush plaque off your teeth, it hardens into a substance called *tartar* which is like cement and impossible to remove with your toothbrush.

It's possible to get dandruff in your eyebrows as well as in the hair on top of your head.

Chewing gum and using straws both make you burp more as they encourage you to swallow air.

A facelift to remove wrinkles involves cutting away part of the skin, pulling the remainder tight again and stitching it in place.

Some people have injections of collagen to 'plump up' their wrinkles. The collagen – a fibre found in skin – is usually taken from pigs or cows.

If you never wear shoes, the skin on the soles of your feet eventually thickens and hardens so that you can walk over sharp stones without hurting yourself.

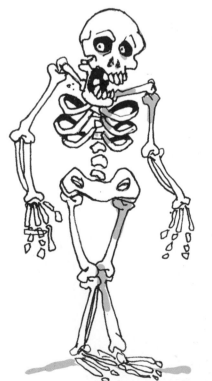

The Bedouin people in the Middle East consider it polite to burp after a meal.

Hair grows all over your body except the palms of your hands, soles of your feet and your lips.

A single drop of blood contains 250 million blood cells.

Vomiting a lot can give you a black eye – the pressure can burst the blood vessels around your eyes.

Romans used to clean their teeth with urine, and it was used as a mouthwash until the 1800s in Europe.

A bruise is bleeding under your skin. The blood can't get out if there isn't a cut, so it just leaks around – it's purple because that's the colour of blood that doesn't have any oxygen in it.

Even a bald person has very fine hair on their head, called *vellus*.

The gunge that collects in your belly button is a mix of dirt, dead skin cells and oils from your body.

If you could line up all your blood cells – all 25 billion of them – they would go round the world four times.

The Binderwur tribe in India used to kill and eat sick and old people to please their goddess Kali.

The medical name for burping is *eructation*.

Your belly button is formed from the shrivelled up stump of the umbilical cord – the tube that connected you to your mother's body before you were born.

Over a ton of pubic hair has to be filtered out of London's sewage each year and removed to landfill sites.

Most people fart about 14 times a day.

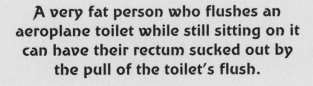

A very fat person who flushes an aeroplane toilet while still sitting on it can have their rectum sucked out by the pull of the toilet's flush.

At any one time, parasites account for one-hundredth of your body weight.

Human hair grows about just over a centimetre (half an inch) a month.

Air you swallow, and gas released from food as you digest it, comes out as a burp or a fart – which one depends on how far through your intestines it has got.

The best recorded distance for projectile vomiting is 8 metres (27 feet)!

Expert botfly squeezers (employed to remove botfly maggots from people) can shoot a botfly from an infected swelling distances of 3 metres (10 feet) or more.

When you die, the bacteria in your gut start to eat away at you from the inside.

The botfly lays its eggs on a mosquito, and they hatch when the mosquito bites someone. The maggot grows for six weeks in a lump under the persons' skin called a warble until it pops out when it's fully grown.

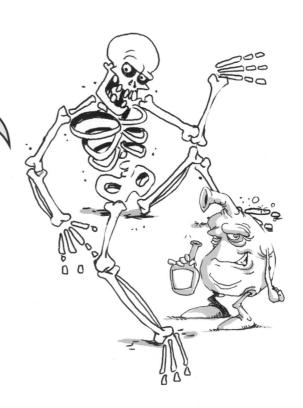

A man with the stage name of Enigma has had surgery to give him horns on his head. He is hoping to get a tail sometime in the future.

In some parts of the world, people wear extremely heavy ear-rings to weigh their ears down and stretch the lobes. They can weigh up to half a kilogram (1 pound) and hang from huge, long holes in the ear lobe.

You swallow about 2 pints of mucus (snot) every day.

Rhinotillexomania is the scientific word for picking your nose.

When you breathe normally, air goes into your nose at about 6.5 kilometres (4 miles) per hour. When you take a good sniff at something, it goes in at 32 kilometres (20 miles) per hour. When you sneeze, it comes out at 160 kilometres (100 miles) per hour!

A scab forms because cells in your blood called platelets make a very thin fibre that traps other blood cells and holds them in a layer that dries out over a scratch or cut.

If you could lay out all your blood vessels end to end they would go round the world over twice.

> **The mental disorder called 'walking corpse' disease leads people to believe parts of their body are missing or that they are dead.**

There is enough iron in the human body to make a nail.

Your body absorbs about two-thirds of the volume of the food you eat – the rest is squished into faeces.

> **Hookworms can infest people who walk barefoot. They bore through the skin of the feet and travel in the blood to the lungs, where they come out and crawl up to the throat, to be swallowed and start a new life in the gut.**

A dead body quickly looks greyish as the blood drains down to the part of the body closest to the ground. The effect is most noticeable in people with white skin.

Right-handed people sweat most under their right arm, left-handed people sweat most under their left arm.

People who live in big cities make more ear wax than those who live in the country, where the air is cleaner.

Nearly half the dust in your house – and that vacuumed up when you clean the house – is old skin cells!

Your intestines are about four times your height – they fit because they're all squashed up and coiled around.

An adult has around 5 million hairs on their head and body.

The infection thrush causes a white, hairy fungus to grow on the tongue.

Nose-pickings are a mix of drying mucus and rubbish filtered out of the air you breathe in – pollen, dust, smoke, dirt, sand, and even tiny particles of dust from space!

The skin of an adult laid out flat on the floor would cover about 1.67 square metres (18 square feet).

Dandruff is a mixture of dirt and dead skin cells stuck together with oil that oozes out of your glands on your head. If your head oozes too much oil, your dandruff becomes noticeable.

Babies can get extra thick, yellow dandruff that sticks to their heads in scales. It's called cradle cap and is more noticeable because they usually don't have much hair.

The toilet paper that Americans use in one day would go around the world nine times.

A person produces 1.5 litres (2.6 pints) of spit (saliva) every day and swallows almost all of it.

You lose 80 hairs from your head every day – but you have about 100,000 so don't worry, you won't start to look bald just yet. And they re-grow quickly when you're young.

Your heart pumps around 182 million litres (48 million gallons) of blood in your lifetime – with an endless supply of blood, it could fill a swimming pool in less than a month!

Beards grow faster than any other body hair. If a man never cut his beard, it would grow 9.1 metres (30 feet) in his lifetime.

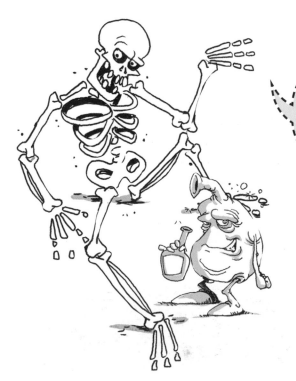

If you could spread out your lungs on the ground, unravelling all the tiny little pockets, they would cover a tennis court.

When you sneeze, all your body functions stop – even your heart stops beating. A very long sneezing fit can cause a heart attack.

When you blush, your stomach blushes, too! A blush sends blood flooding into the tiny blood vessels on your face and also to the many blood vessels inside your stomach.

The longest tape worm ever found in a human was 33 metres (around 108 feet) long.

When you vomit, the same muscle movements that push food down through your gut go into reverse, pushing it back up again.

It can take up to two days for food to pass through your body – from going in your mouth to coming out your bottom.

A spot or pimple is caused by a waxy oil called *sebum* and tiny bits of dead skin collecting in a little hole in your skin. It goes black if it gets big enough to force your pore open and let air in. When bacteria start to eat away at the gunk, a red spot with nasty yellow pus inside grows.

One in 100,000 people is born with an extra finger on each hand, but usually they are only small stumps.

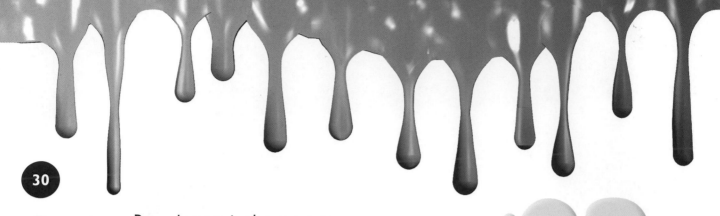

Roundworm is the most common gut parasite in the world. It looks rather like an earthworm, and you can catch it by eating food contaminated with faeces.

A smelly fart contains the same gas that makes rotten eggs stink – *hydrogen sulphide*.

If you laid out the airways in your lungs in a long line they would stretch over 2,400 kilometres (1,500 miles).

If too much wax builds up in your ears, a doctor can soften it and then scoop it out with a special spoon called a *curette*.

Danish astronomer Tyco Brahe wore a metal nose because his own fell off after he suffered from the disease *syphilis*.

Sometimes, if a person's eye comes out of its socket in an accident and dangles on their cheek, they can push it back in with no lasting ill effects – don't try it at home!

When you sleep, you aren't blinking so there is no way to sweep away the mix of water, oils and other chemicals that wash over your eyes. Instead, they dry out around the edges of your eyes making crispy or slimy yellow gunk.

Sweat doesn't actually smell – it's the bacteria breaking it down that produce the pong.

Most people produce around 1.7 litres (3 pints) of urine a day.

Wet hair stretches to about 1.5 times its dry length.

The sores caused by the disease *typhus* can rot the flesh, sometimes causing toes and fingers to drop off.

If you took all the nerves out of an adult's body and laid them end to end they would stretch 75 kilometres (47 miles). But the adult would not be pleased.

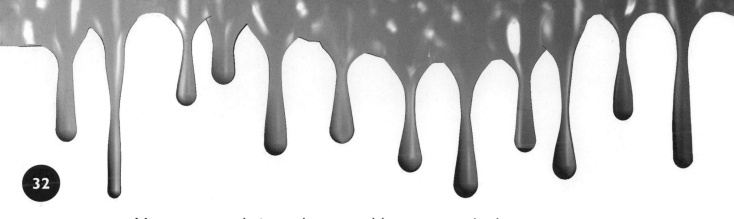

Men grow ear hair as they get older; women don't.

Food can slosh around in your stomach for up to 4 hours, churning around like a washing machine.

Feet smell really bad sometimes because lots of bacteria and fungi like to live on them – especially if they are hot and wet and sweaty. The bacteria feed on the dead skin and sweat making smelly gases.

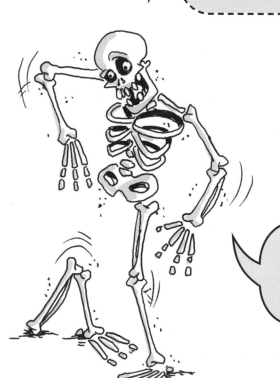

If you have a spitting contest, you'll do better if you can see some food, or even a picture of food. If you can't manage that, just thinking about your favourite food will help to make your mouth water.

If you throw up and your vomit is greenish, it contains bile from further down in your intestine than just your stomach. The bile and stomach acid make vomit taste awful.

The disease *necrotising fasciitis* causes the flesh to rot from within and drop off in chunks. Holes up to 15 centimetres (6 inches) across can form in sufferers' bodies.

Your eyes make 4.5 litres (8 pints) of tears a year – they keep your eyes wet even if you're not crying.

Slime oozes from the inside of your stomach to stop the acid in the stomach dissolving its walls and eating into your body – digesting you from the inside.

A gut parasite carried in water infested half a million people in Wisconsin in 1993 when it got into the water supply. A hundred people died.

Stomach gurgling – called *borborygmus* by scientists – is the sound of half-digested food, gas and stomach acid churning around.

After you die, your body starts to dry out and shrink, creating the illusion that your hair and nails are still growing after death.

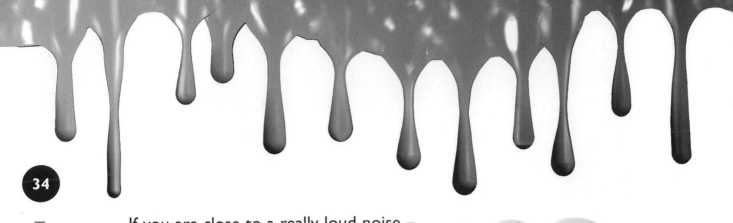

If you are close to a really loud noise – a massive volcano erupting, or a huge explosion – the thin, tight skin inside your ear called your eardrum can burst with the pressure.

To save space, 98 percent of dead Japanese people are cremated rather than buried.

There are more germs under your fingernails than on a toilet seat.

When you sneeze, up to a million tiny viruses are sprayed out of your nose and mouth. Just one of these can be enough to infect someone else.

Babies are born without kneecaps – they develop at between two to six years of age.

In Palestine, pregnant women who hoped for a son used to drink a potion made from the burned and powdered umbilical cord of a new-born baby boy.

Urine doesn't smell until it hits the air. Then a chemical in it called *urea* starts to break down into *ammonia* and the smell begins...

Chinese leader Mao Tse Tung never brushed his teeth, giving as a reason that tigers never brushed their teeth either.

William McIlloy had 400 operations because he suffered from Munchausen's Syndrome, which is a mental disorder that makes people want to receive medical treatment. He had to give a false name and move around a lot to get away with it.

People either have pale and dry or dark and sticky ear wax. It's an inherited trait, with dry earwax more common in Asia, or people of Asian decent.

Faeces smells largely because the microbes in your gut produce two stinky chemicals as they work to break down your food – *indole* and *skatole*.

Two thousand glands in your ear make ear wax to protect you from getting dirt, dust and germs deep in your ear. The wax slowly hardens and comes to the edge of your ear to fall out. If it doesn't fall out, it can harden into a plug of wax up to 2.5 centimetres (about 1 inch) long.

Before artificial false teeth were made of porcelain in the 1800s, many people who needed false teeth wore teeth pulled from the mouths of corpses.

The weight of ashes from the average cremated human body is 4 kilograms (9 pounds).

King Louis IV of France had a stomach twice the size of a normal human stomach.

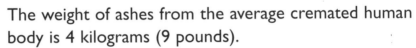

A French entertainer in the late 1800s used to make 'music' by farting out tunes.

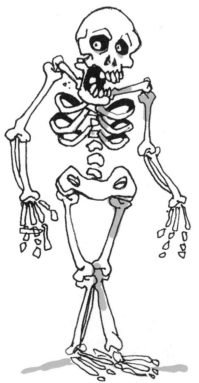

A man with the stage name 'Lizardman' has slit his tongue in two, from the tip to the middle, so that it is forked. He also has green scales tattooed over his skin.

You shed and regrow your skin roughly every 27 days, making a total of around 1,000 complete skins in a lifetime. A person who lives to 70 years of age will shed 47.6 kilograms (105 pounds) of skin.

A newborn baby produces its own body weight in faeces every 60 hours.

It takes just over 3 kilograms (7 pounds) of pressure to tear off a human ear – don't try it!

King Louis XIV of France's feet started to rot in his old age. A valet found a toe that dropped off in one of the king's socks.

There is enough fat in the human body to make seven bars of soap.

When you have diarrhoea, instead of absorbing water from your food, your intestines ooze more water into it to rush it through the system and out the other end as a watery mush.

Queen Isabella of Spain boasted that she only took two baths in her whole-life – one when she was born, and one before her wedding.

There are more bacteria in your mouth than there are people in the world.

Ear wax comes in a range of colours including yellow, grey, brown and pumpkin-orange.

An adult human contains enough water to fill three large buckets.

It would take 20 minutes to pour all the human urine produced in a single day over the Niagara Falls.

If your head is chopped off, you can remain conscious for about 25 seconds!

If your fingers or toes get very cold, they can get frostbite. They slowly rot and go black, and have to be cut off to stop the rot spreading.

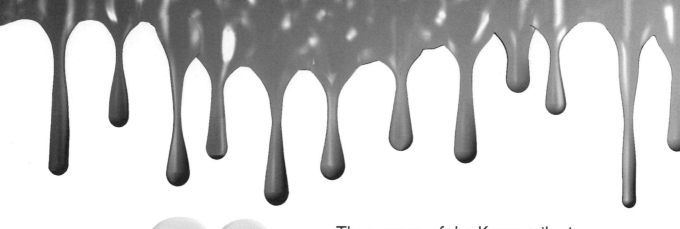

Electric signals from the brain can continue for 37 hours after death.

The women of the Karen tribe in Thailand traditionally wear masses of metal bands around their necks. The first bands are added on a girl's fifth birthday, and more are added every few months. If the bands are removed, the woman's weakened neck can't support her head. Removing the bands became an effective punishment.

While talking, we spit out 300 tiny drops of spit per minute.

In Scandinavian countries, people used to burn children's first teeth when they fell out in case witches found them and used them to cast an evil spell on the child.

The scabies mite burrows inside your skin making long tunnels and causing horrible itching.

There is enough sulphur in a human body to kill all the fleas on a dog.

The energy from the food you need in one day is just enough to heat four teaspoons of water from freezing point to boiling.

Every minute, 30,000–40,000 skin cells drop off your body.

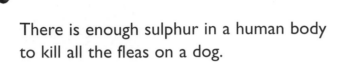

Godfrey Hill, from the UK, has ten complete fingers and two thumbs, and has been accused of being an alien or the Messiah.

If you try to stop yourself from throwing up by closing your mouth, the vomit will just come out of your nose.

You will produce about 33,000 litres (8,700 gallons) of urine in your life.

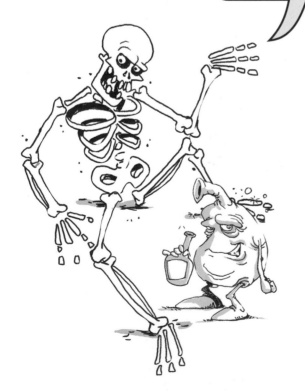

Horrible
Food Facts

Bedouin wedding feasts sometimes include a roast camel, stuffed with a sheep, stuffed with chickens, stuffed with fish, stuffed with eggs.

In the 1800s, it was common to mix ground bones into flour to make it go further.

Henry V of England once held a Christmas feast at which the menu included carps' tongues, roasted dolphin and flowers set in jelly.

An average-sized person eats around 22,700 kilograms (50,000 pounds) of food over the course of their life.

Honey is bee vomit. Bees drink nectar from flowers which they turn into honey before sicking it back up to store in the hive.

Flavours of ice-cream available in Japan include octopus, ox tongue, cactus, chicken wing and crab.

The Roman emperor Nero kept a 'glutton' – an Egyptian slave who ate everything he was given to eat, including human flesh.

To make especially tender beef, the Japanese shut cattle in the dark, feed them beer and employ special cattle masseurs to massage them by hand three times a day.

Stink-heads are a traditional Alaskan dish. Fish heads – often from salmon – are buried in pits lined with moss for a few weeks or months until rotten. They are then kneaded like pastry to mix up all the parts and eaten.

Argentinian Gauchos keep a piece of beef under their saddles so that it is pummelled until tender as they ride around all day. It's said that the dish steak tartar came from Mongolian warriors doing the same and then eating the steak raw.

The Spanish eat the cheese *cabrales* when it is 'con gusano' – crawling with live maggots.

In India, ants are roasted, ground to a paste and served as chutney.

A stew eaten at a funeral in Stone-Age Wales was made from shellfish, eels, mice, frogs, toads, shrews and snakes.

In Sardinia, cheese is left in the sun for flies to lay their egg in. When the maggots hatch, the swarming mass is spread on bread and eaten.

An eighteenth-century recipe for making an enormous egg suggests sewing 20 egg yolks into an animal bladder, then dropping it into another animal bladder filled with 20 egg whites and boiling it all together.

In 1919, a tidal wave of treacle swept through Boston, USA. A storage tank burst, spilling 7.5 million litres (2 million gallons) of it into the streets. It poured over houses, knocking them down, in a wave two storeys high.

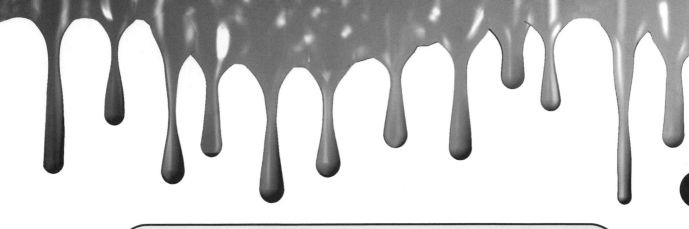

During the Second World War, people in the UK were urged by the government to make the most of wild foods, and were given recipes for cooking roast squirrel, rook casserole, stewed starlings and baked sparrows.

Odd crisp flavours available around the world include octopus, seaweed, banana, and sour cream and squid.

The Insect Club, a restaurant in the USA, serves only dishes made with insects. The menu includes cricket pizza, insect chocolates and 'insects in a blanket' – crickets, mealworms and blue cheese in puff pastry.

In 1971, a man found the head of a mouse in a bar of chocolate.

Condemned prisoners are traditionally allowed a delicious last meal. In some US states, it's not actually their last meal, but is served a day or two before the execution and is called a 'special meal'.

Tradition tells that the French cheese Roquefort was discovered when a shepherd abandoned his lunch in a cave to chase a pretty girl he saw outside. When he came back months later the cheese had gone mouldy but still tasted good.

Durian is a fruit the size of a football, covered in spikes, that smells like rotting meat. It's supposed to taste good, though!

Roman banquets often featured hummingbirds cooked in walnut shells and roasted stuffed dormice, sometimes rolled in honey and poppy seeds. The Romans even had farms producing dormice because they were so popular.

In Slovenia, people still raise and fatten dormice, ready to stew.

In Nepal, Tibet and parts of China, black tea is served with yak butter – butter made from yak milk.

During the First World War, Germany suffered such food shortages that people ate dogs and horses, and even the kangaroos from the zoos!

Raake orret is eaten in Norway. Trout caught in a fresh water stream are stored in salted water with a little sugar and kept in a cool place, such as the garage, for months before eating.

P'tcha is an east European Jewish food made by stewing calves' feet until they turn to jelly.

Ambuyat, eaten in Brunei, is made from pulp from the sago palm, stewed in water for several hours. The same mixture is made to stick the roof on a house!

Also in Brunei, the sago worm which lives inside rotting sago palms is often cooked and eaten.

In Northern Australia, children often eat green ants. Pick them up, squish the head so they don't nibble you, and bite off the body.

In Madagascar, people make a stew from tomatoes and zebras.

Pruno is a 'wine' made by American prisoners from a mixture of fruit, sugar cubes, water and tomato ketchup left to fester in a bin bag for a week. In some prisons, pruno causes so many discipline problems that fruit has been banned.

A restaurant in Osaka, Japan, serves whale ice-cream made from the blubber of the minke whale.

In the Japanese countryside, salamanders and skinks are grilled on sticks and served with lettuce.

In Nicaragua, turtle eggs are eaten raw – slit the leathery skin, add some hot sauce and suck out the gunk.

Cinemas in Colombia serve paper cones filled with giant fried or toasted ants.

A rat restaurant in China sells rat and snake soup, rat kebabs, steamed rat with rice and crispy fried rat.

In Newfoundland, Canada, seal flipper pie is a traditional dish for the end of a seal hunt.

A restaurant in Changsha, China, offers food cooked in human breast milk.

Think cabbage is horrid? In Korea, it is sometimes buried in clay pots with salt for many months before it's eaten – this dish is called *kimchi,* and is served with most meals.

Alligator kebabs are popular in southern Louisiana, USA.

In Fiji, people starve a pig for a week, then feed it veal when it is very hungry. A few hours later, they kill the pig and remove the half-digested veal, which they cook and eat.

In Texas, there's an annual rattle-snake round-up. What to do with all the rattle snakes? Skin them, gut them, cut them into chunks, cover in batter and deep fry.

Another way of cooking snakes in Texas — cut the head off, skin and gut it, poke a stick into the neck, wrap the snake loosely around the stick and roast over a camp fire.

In China, people eat jellied ducks' blood.

Iguanas are a popular and free food in Central America — they can often be caught in backyards.

Slimy green stuff that looks like mucus is supposedly the best part of a lobster or crayfish. It's found in the head. Some Americans eat the main part of the lobster meat and then suck the head to get the gunge out.

As early as the ninth century, the Basques of Spain hunted whales, and whale tongue was considered a great delicacy.

Oellebroed is a Danish soup make from stale rye bread soaked in water, then boiled with beer and sugar and served with cream. It's possible to buy instant oellebroed powder — just add water.

Cibreo is an Italian dish that consists of the cooked combs from roosters.

Spam is a luncheon meat used as a filling for sandwiches. At a Spam-cooking contest, one contestant made Spam-chip cookies!

In Canada, deep-fried cod tongues are a popular dish.

The street markets of Indonesia sell whole, smoked bats.

McDonald's in Hong Kong sells a sweetcorn pie in a sweet pie crust, the same as the apple pies in the west.

An international contest to find the best recipe for cooking earthworms included entries of stews, salads and soups but was won by a recipe for applesauce surprise cake. Guess what the surprise was…

Baby mouse wine, from China, is a bottle of wine packed with baby mice, to add flavour.

Jack Fuller was buried in a pyramid in Sussex, England, in 1811. It's said by local people that inside it he is seated at a table with a roast chicken and a bottle of port.

Some Arctic explorers have been poisoned by eating polar bear liver. The polar bear eats so much fish that fatal levels of Vitamin D collect in its liver.

A restaurant in Pennsylvania, USA, offers a hamburger that weighs 4 kilograms (9 pounds). No one has yet managed to finish one.

The Chinese make a soup from the swim bladder of fish. It's the organ that helps fish to stay at the right depth and upright in the water, and is rather spongy.

Drunken shrimps, served in China, are live shrimps swimming in a bowl of rice wine. The idea is to catch them with chopsticks and bite the heads off.

Bedouin people cook a camel's hump by burying it underground and lighting a fire over the top of it. When they dig it up and eat it, the top is cooked, but the bottom still mostly raw and bloody.

In Ness, Scotland, people kill young gannets – a type of sea bird – to eat. The claws are the most highly prized part.

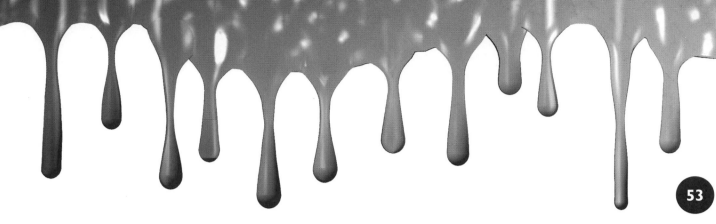

Crispy fried duck or chicken feet are a delicacy in China. In the USA, whole chicken feet are sometimes pickled or made into soup.

Eskimos have been known to make seagull wine – put a seagull in a bottle of water, wait for it to go off – drink!

In both Sicily and Japan, people eat the raw roe (eggs) of sea urchins.

In the Philippines, the eyes are considered the tastiest part of a steamed fish. Suck out the gloop and spit out the hard cornea.

Fried chicken cartilage is served as a bar snack in Japan.

Marmite, a favourite English spread for toast, is made with the left-over yeasty sludge from brewing beer.

Snake wine in China is a very potent alcoholic drink, spiced with juice from the gall bladder of a live snake.

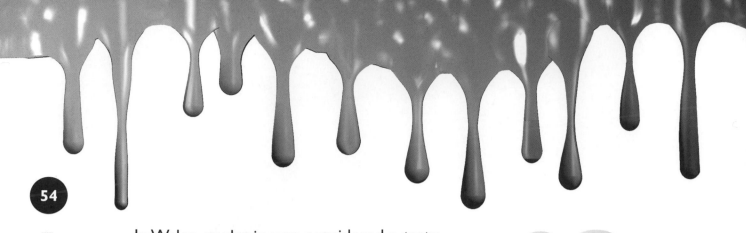

In Wales, rook pie was considered a tasty way to get rid of a bird that might otherwise eat the crops.

Nutria are a large rodent that live some of the time in the water. They are a pest in Louisiana, where local authorities are encouraging people to eat them – with little success, as they don't taste too good.

A traditional dish in London is eels boiled and served cold in jelly.

In the southern USA, squirrel brains are cooked still in the head. You then crack the skull and scoop the brains out with fingers and fork.

In Hungary, scrambled eggs are fried up with the blood from a freshly slaughtered pig.

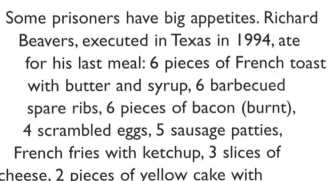

Some prisoners have big appetites. Richard Beavers, executed in Texas in 1994, ate for his last meal: 6 pieces of French toast with butter and syrup, 6 barbecued spare ribs, 6 pieces of bacon (burnt), 4 scrambled eggs, 5 sausage patties, French fries with ketchup, 3 slices of cheese, 2 pieces of yellow cake with chocolate fudge icing and 4 cartons of milk.

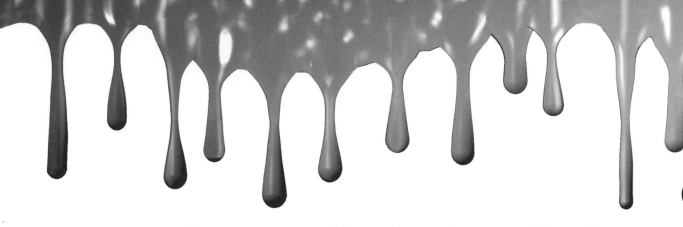

Biltong is favoured as a snack by rugby supporters in South Africa. It's dried strips of any meat – elephant, eland, antelope…

In Indonesia, deep fried monkey toes are eaten by sucking the meat straight off the bone.

In Sweden, people make dumplings from flour, reindeer blood and salt.

In Japan, the blowfish is a delicacy, even though it contains a poison gland which, if not properly removed, kills anyone who eats it.

An omelette costing $1000 (£530) and called the Zillion Dollar Lobster Frittata was sold by a restaurant in New York. It contains a whole lobster and 280 grams (10 ounces) of caviar, as well as eggs, cream, potato and whiskey.

In Georgia, there is a price limit of $20 on the last meal a prisoner can order (2004 price limit).

Small songbirds cooked and eaten whole have been so popular in Italy that many types have been wiped out completely.

In Sweden and Norway, roast reindeer is a national dish.

Many cheap meat products such as sausages and burgers are made from 'mechanically recovered meat' which consists of a meat slurry collected from washing bones and mincing up parts of the dead animal that aren't used for anything else.

In the Philippines, chicken heads may be made into stew or barbecued whole.

Jellyfish are eaten dried and salted in some parts of the world. And in the Gilbert Islands, jellyfish ovaries are served fried.

Aztecs gave people who were to be human sacrifices many last meals — they fattened them up for up to a year.

The Russian Jewish dish *kishke* is made by stuffing a chicken skin with flour, butter and spices and boiling it in chicken stock. Dry it out, then cut it into slices as a snack.

In China and Japan, sheets of dried jellyfish are sold for soaking and turning back into slimy jellyfish ready for cooking.

Ancient Greeks, Egyptians and Romans all gave condemned prisoners a last meal.

The Chinese eat monster barnacles the size of an adult's fist.

The reproductive organs of sea urchins are eaten raw in many parts of the world, including Japan, Chile and France.

The town of Bunol, in Spain, has an annual tomato fight when up to 25,000 people throw around 100 tonnes (220,000 pounds) of tomatoes at each other. The streets can be flooded up to 30 centimetres (12 inches) deep with juice.

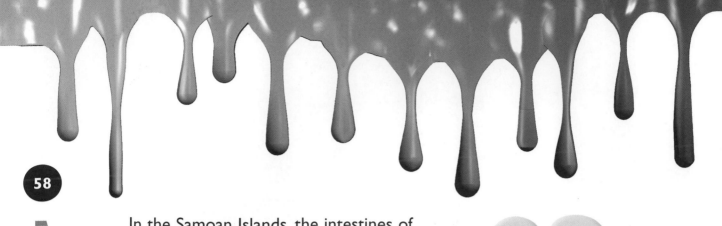

In the Samoan Islands, the intestines of sea cucumbers are sold in jars, steeped in sea water. The sea cucumber is a slithery, tube-like animal and not a cucumber at all. When it's cooked, it is called a sea slug.

In the UK, game – wild animals and birds shot in the fields – is often hung until it is 'high', which means it is hung up on a hook until it is starting to go off.

The alcoholic drink *mescal* has a cactus maggot preserved in the bottle.

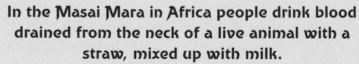

In the Masai Mara in Africa people drink blood drained from the neck of a live animal with a straw, mixed up with milk.

Raw, pickled jellyfish are eaten in the Samoan Islands.

Yeast are tiny fungi (mould), present in bread, beer and wine. The yeast eat sugar in the ingredients, making the gas which forms the bubbles in beer and wine and the holes in bread.

Eels are sold live in markets around the world and killed just before cooking – or before putting in the bag to go home, if you don't want the bag wriggling all the way.

Orangutan lips used to be a delicacy in Vietnam.

The British black pudding is a sausage made of congealed pigs' blood with lumps of fat embedded in it. It is often fried and eaten for breakfast.

Soft ice-cream of the type sold in ice-cream vans is given its slithery smoothness by an extract of seaweed.

Baby eels, called elvers, are eaten in parts of Europe, including east England. They are very thin, so lots are cooked, tangled together like spaghetti.

In France, calves' eyes are soaked in water, then boiled and stuffed and finally deep fried in breadcrumbs.

Most US states don't allow alcohol or tobacco in a prisoner's last meal.

Cow's tongue is often sold with the salivary glands – the parts that make spit – ready for boiling. The tongue can weigh up to 2.3 kilograms (5 pounds).

In Europe, some people make blood pudding from the blood of a pig or cow mixed with rice, milk and sugar and then baked.

To make the expensive *pate de foie gras*, geese are forcibly fattened with grain so that their liver swells to many times its natural size.

In England, lampreys – a fierce fish that looks like an eel – are traditionally cooked in a sauce flavoured with their own blood.

In Mexico, the alcoholic drink tequila is often served with a worm in the glass – the worm should be swallowed whole with the drink.

Romany people in Europe, and poor peasants, used to cook wild hedgehogs by rolling them in mud and baking them in the embers of a fire. When the mud dries, the spines can be peeled off with the mud.

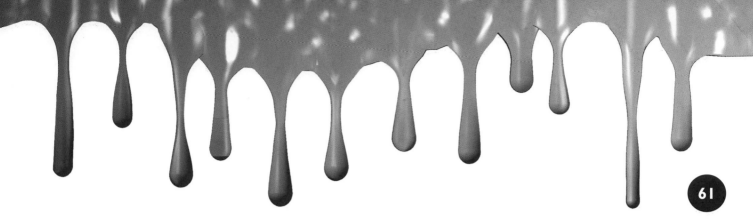

Roast dog is sold on the streets of Vietnam. The back half of the dog comes with the tail intact.

Caviar is the eggs of the sturgeon fish. It is so valuable that an operation is sometimes used to remove the eggs without harming the fish, which then goes on to make more eggs. Previously, the fish was gutted while still alive so that the eggs could be as fresh as possible.

In Central and South America, iguana meat is highly prized.

The French *cervela* sausage is made with the brains of pigs.

Mealworms – golden-coloured larvae that eat grain – are farmed in the USA and sold live in pots of bran for cooking. The bran is for the meal-worm to eat while they are waiting, as otherwise they will eat each other.

Sheep's eyeballs are eaten in some Arab countries of North Africa.

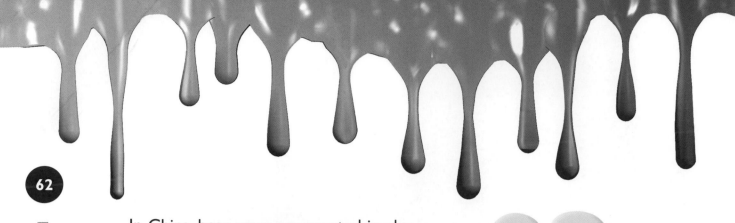

In China, bear paws are roasted in clay – the fur comes off with the dried clay when they are done.

In France, rats found in wine cellars were sometimes cooked in a sauce flavoured with red wine, over a fire of burning wine barrels.

The Aztec dish *tlacatalalli* was a stew made from corn and human beings.

In the 1800s, naturalist Frank Buckland served meals such as mice on toast, roasted parrots and stewed sea slug. He tried to make soup from an elephant's trunk, but even after several days' cooking it was still too chewy.

Birds nest soup is a delicacy in China. It's made from the nests of a special variety of swift that builds its nest from dried strands of its own spit. The nest is soaked in water to soften it, then any sticks and feathers are removed before it is made into a gluey, sticky soup.

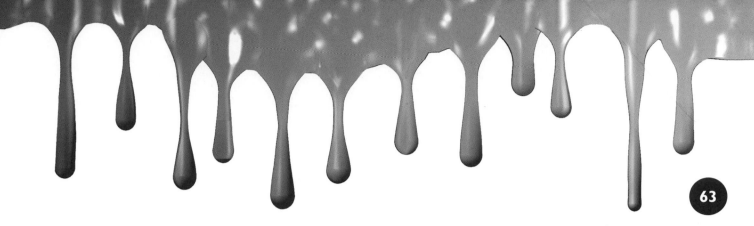

Truffles are a kind of fungus that grow underground in forests in Europe. Truffle hunters use pigs to smell them out. The best truffles are extremely valuable.

In the Middle Ages, a peacock was often roasted with its feathers on. The skin was inflated first to stop the feathers burning, and then pierced when the bird was cooked so that it appeared as though it were alive when served.

Some Amazonian tribes used to make a soup with the ground bones of their dead relatives.

Once, at a Roman banquet, a slave stabbed the stomach of a roast boar to release a flock of live thrushes.

In Texas, armadillos are sometimes roasted in their shells, stuffed with carrots, apples and potatoes.

The Akoa pygmy tribe eat elephant meat with a serving of live maggots.

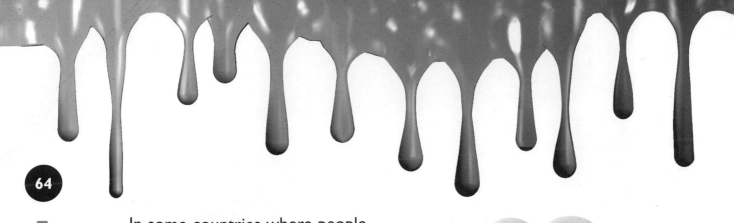

1001 Horrible Facts

In some countries where people don't have food processors or forks, mothers chew up food to put into their babies' mouths.

Some Jewish people eat the braised udder of a cow.

Worms steamed whole in a jelly are a tasty treat in China.

The oldest surviving piece of chewing gum is 9,000 years old.

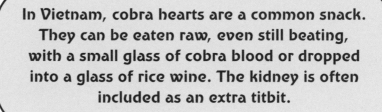

In Vietnam, cobra hearts are a common snack. They can be eaten raw, even still beating, with a small glass of cobra blood or dropped into a glass of rice wine. The kidney is often included as an extra titbit.

US Airforce pilot, Captain Scott O'Grady, was shot down over Bosnia in 1995 and survived for six days eating only ants.

In 1135, King Henry I of England died from eating too many lampreys – a kind of eel that sucks its victims to death.

Eel skin is so hard to remove that some people pull it off with pliers.

Camels' feet are cooked in a light stock and served with vinaigrette. Only the feet of young camels are considered tasty.

Camel feet can also be cooked in camel milk.

The original recipe for baked beans included bear fat and maple syrup.

The Scottish dish haggis is made by cutting up the heart, lungs, liver and small intestine of a calf or sheep and cooking it with suet, oatmeal, onions and herbs in the animal's stomach.

Australian aborigines like to eat witchetty grubs – the larvae of the ghost moth – raw and wriggling. Or they can be barbecued on wire for a couple of minutes, like a kebab.

A restaurant in England recently offered snail porridge on its menu.

In the Faroe Islands, a favourite dish is puffin stuffed with rhubarb.

In China, eggs are buried underground until they go exceptionally bad and are then sold and eaten as 'hundred-year-old' eggs. In fact, they are about two years old. The yolks turn green and the whites turn grey or black.

In China, sharks' fin soup is made from the salted, sun-dried fins of sharks. It is like a bowl of glue, as the fin contains a lot of gelatine.

People in ancient China ate mice as a delicacy.

Roman feasts sometimes included the popular delicacy flamingo tongues.

For his last meal, murderer Victor Feguer chose a single olive.

Honey found in ancient Egyptian tombs has been tasted by archaeologists and found to be edible still, after thousands of years.

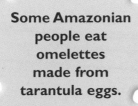

Some Amazonian people eat omelettes made from tarantula eggs.

If you eat too many carrots, you will turn orange.

Fried crickets are a favourite food in China.

The Japanese make *natto* by leaving soy beans to rot in straw until slimy and sticky – and very smelly.

The Air Force Survival Manual issued to US airmen explains which bugs to eat in an emergency for maximum taste and nutrition.

The last meal of Oklahoma Bomber Timothy McVeigh was almost a litre (2 pints) of mint choc-chip ice-cream.

Australian supermarkets sell tins of witchetty grub soup.

In France, over 40,000 metric tons (88 million pounds) of snails are consumed every year.

Mealworms are supposed to taste better if cooked while still alive.

Sea slug is eaten in China and Spain. It's often sold dried and has to be soaked to restore it to its slimy, squishy glory.

Blood soup is popular in many parts of the world. In Poland, people eat a duck blood soup called *czarnina*; in Korea, pig blood curd soup is called *seonjiguk*; and in the Philippines people eat a pig blood stew called *dinuguan*.

Iowa State University's Department of Entomology has published recipes for cooking with insects, including banana worm bread, crackers and cheese dip with candied crickets and mealworm fried rice.

Sun-dried maggots have been eaten from China to North America.

In Ghana, half of the locally produced meat comes from rats.

Central American wedding feasts often included honeyed ants.

When a pig is roasted in Cuba, the skull is cracked open and each guest takes a spoon to share scoops of brain.

In 1973, a Swedish sweets salesman was buried in a coffin made of chocolate.

In Mexico, a black fungus which infects maize is canned and sold. It looks like black slime with a few yellow lumps in.

Water cockroaches are roasted and eaten in China — leave the wings and legs.

The Korean delicacy *sannakji* consists of still-wriggling slices of octopus tentacle.

In the Philippines, fertilized duck or chicken eggs are cooked and eaten – with the unhatched chick partly grown inside. It's called *balut*, in case you want to avoid it on the menu.

Oysters are always eaten raw – alive – in the UK and USA.

In Cambodia, giant grilled spiders are a popular street snack.

An American delicacy called headcheese, similar to British brawn, is made by cooking a whole cow or pig head into a mush and letting it cool into a jelly-like mass.

In China, people get their own back on poisonous scorpions by frying them. They are said to taste rather like cashew nuts.

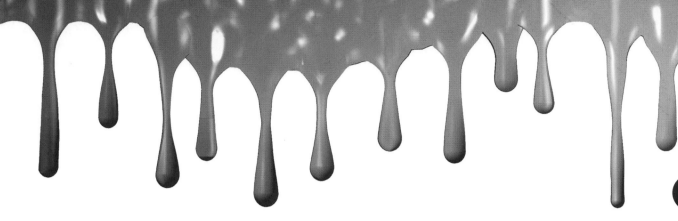

Until 1999, it was legal to enjoy ortolan in France – a tiny, rare, song bird, fattened in a dark box to three times it normal size then drowned in brandy and spit roasted for a few minutes before being eaten whole, innards included. (It was OK to leave the head and beak.) Traditionally, it was eaten with a napkin draped over your head and the plate so that none of the delicious smell could escape.

Native Alaskan Indians bury salmon eggs in a jar for ninety days and eat them when they are truly rotten.

In Finland, people cook blood pancakes.

Kakambian, from the Philippines, is made of diced goat – skin, hair, fat and meat all mixed together.

Delicacies enjoyed in Iceland include puffin and *svie* – singed and boiled sheep's head.

In some parts of Asia, monkey brains are a delicacy – but it's a myth that they are eaten from the head while the monkey is still alive.

> In Mongolia, camel or horse milk is stored in a cleaned horse stomach or hide bag and hung up in the *ger* (tent). Everyone who passes the door has to stir or hit the bag. It slowly ferments into a slightly alcoholic, cheesy, yoghurt drink which everyone drinks, even children.

At the winter festival of Thorrablot, Icelanders eat *hákarl* – rotten shark. Shark meat is buried in the ground for six to eight weeks then dried in the open air for two months.

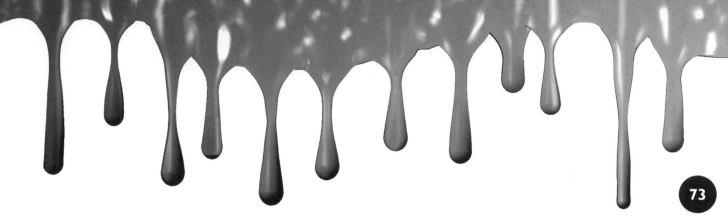

Bagoong is a very smelly, fermented paste made from mashed shrimps and eaten in the Philippines.

In Palau, whole fruit bats, complete with skin, may be ordered as a starter or main course.

In southern Africa, large caterpillars called *mopani* can be bought in tins.

Morcilla is a Puerto Rican sausage made with rice boiled in pigs' blood, stuffed into a sausage skin and then fried.

In Ecuador, a family barbecue can include guinea pig and snake kebabs.

In north Africa, people eat fried termites.

In Brazil, people eat barbecued armadillo.

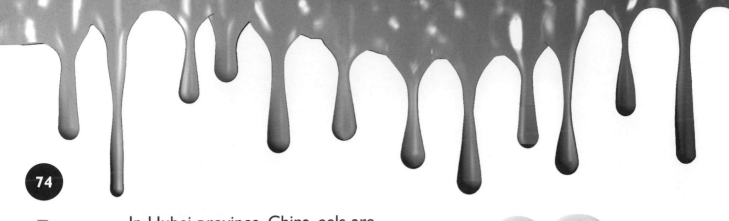

In Hubei province, China, eels are served whole. The correct way to eat one is to bite though just behind the head and pull out the insides with chopsticks.

In Hong Kong, you can buy packets of crispy fried crabs like packets of crisps.

Rocky Mountain oysters, or prairie oysters, are calves' testicles – enjoyed fried in parts of the USA.

The Japanese dish *shiokara* is made by fermenting squid in old fish guts.

In some rural parts of China, you can get owl soup.

In Korea, it's possible to buy canned silk worm pupae, or bags of silkworm from street vendors. The idea is to crunch the end off the grub and suck out the juices.

Spider wine, from Cambodia, is actually rice wine – the spiders are added later.

Horrible
Animal Facts

The pearl fish swims into a sea cucumber's anus and lives inside it in the day time, coming out at night. The sea cucumber breathes through its anus, so can't keep the fish out!

The glass frog has a transparent body – its blood vessels, stomach and beating heart are all visible.

A scorpion can go for a whole year without eating.

There are more than 70,000 types of slug and snail in the world. Let's hope they never hold a big party!

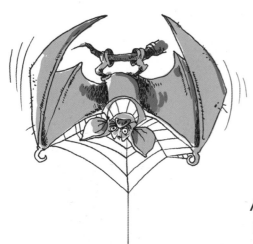

Spiders inject flies and bugs with a chemical which paralyzes them and dissolves their insides. The spider then sucks out the liquid as it can't chew.

As cockroaches grow, they develop a new skin inside their old one, eventually splitting the old one. This new skin is white until it hardens in the air and becomes dark.

The viperfish has teeth so long it can't close its mouth and it has to open its jaws out flat before it can swallow. Its teeth are half the length of its head!

A mosquito can drink one and a half times its own weight in blood at a single meal. Yuk!

The skin of a hippopotamus measures about 4 centimetres (1.5 inches) thick. That's about 3.5 centimetres (over an inch) thicker than human skin.

Bone-eating zombie worms live on the decaying bodies of dead whales. They have no gut, but bore deeply into the bones. Microbes inside the worms digest chemicals sucked out of the bones.

The banded tenrec, a kind of hedgehog from Madagascar, sometimes eats so many worms, bugs and slugs that it makes itself sick.

Sharks will eat almost anything. The stomachs of dead sharks have been found to contain bits of boats and vehicles and even a knight in armour.

If a rat didn't keep chewing, its lower teeth would eventually grow through its top jaw and up into the roof of its mouth.

A shark can taste blood over a kilometre (about half a mile) away.

In the time of the dinosaurs, there were giant scorpions nearly a metre (3 feet) long. That's bigger than the average domestic dog!

Every year, 4.5 million litres (1 million gallons) of dog urine goes into the parks of London, England.

A spider that isn't hungry will wrap up extra bugs in its web to keep for later.

There are 3,500 known species of cockroach. Are there others out there? – we just don't know yet…

Owl's eyes are too large to move in their eye sockets, so they've developed the ability to turn their heads round further than other birds can.

Salamander larvae change form, becoming killer predators, if they sense the vibrations created in water by swimming tadpoles. They grow longer, stronger bodies and broader heads so that they can kill and eat the tadpoles.

Carrying garlic might repel mosquitoes rather than vampires.

Flesh flies eat nothing but old meat and rotting flesh on dead bodies.

A planarian worm will regrow its other half if cut in two. If two planarians are cut in half, they can be mixed up and re-attach to the wrong half.

Geckos have no eyelids — they lick their eyeballs to clean them!

Scorpions glow in the dark in ultraviolet light.

The vampire squid has the largest eyes of any animal for its body size. The squid is 28 centimetres long (11 inches) and its eyes are 2.5 centimetres (1 inch across). The equivalent would be a person with eyes the size of table tennis bats!

The job of guard termites is to defend the termite nest or mound. Sometimes they explode in their efforts to deter attackers.

A duck-billed platypus can stuff its cheek pouches with 600 worms.

A lion's mane jellyfish is about 2.5 metres (8 feet) across, with tentacles 60 metres (200 feet) long. Their sting can cause an agonizing death.

An octopus has to turn itself inside out to eat, as its mouth is hidden in between its tentacles.

The southern giant petrel, a bird which lives near the South Pole, spits globs of oil and regurgitated food at its enemies.

The leopard seal sometimes attacks people, lunging up through the ice to snap at their feet.

The carpet viper kills more people in the world than any other type of snake. Its bite leads to uncontrollable bleeding.

Cockroaches taste through their feet.

A baby naked mole rat has transparent skin – you can see its insides right through its skin!

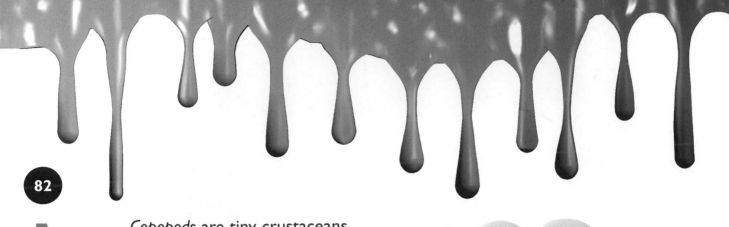

Copepods are tiny crustaceans that swim around in groups of up to a trillion. They are the only known creature that has just one eye.

The wood frog that lives in the Arctic Circle can stay deep-frozen for weeks and survive.

Sharks don't have a urinary tract so their urine leaks out of their skin.

Horses often chew at fly eggs and maggots on their legs and end up swallowing them, so have a stomach full of crawling maggots.

Nose bots are maggots that live inside the noses of animals that graze, such as sheep, cows and horses.

The Gila monster is a lizard from South America and Mexico. Although it's only just over half a metre (2 feet) long, its bite is so strong that the only way to detach one that's bitten you is to drown it.

A rat can fall from a five-storey building and walk away unharmed.

Rats have super-strong teeth. Amongst other things, they can bite through wood, metal and electric cables.

A cockroach can survive being frozen in a block of ice for two days.

The only mammals that don't get lice are anteaters, armadillos, bats, duck-billed platypuses, whales, dolphins and porpoises.

The deep-sea gulper eel can eat fish larger than itself. It can open its mouth so wide that its jaw bends back on itself at an angle of more than 180 degrees.

The caterpillar of the polyphemus moth in North America eats 86,000 times its own birthweight in the first 56 days of its life. It's equal to a human baby eating 270 tonnes (nearly 600,000 pounds) of food!

The bulldog ant from Australia will sting again and again while holding on with its fierce jaws. It can kill a human in 15 minutes.

A pregnant scorpion will sometimes reabsorb its babies instead of giving birth to them.

Mosquitoes in the Arctic hatch when the snows thaw, sometimes making such large swarms they blot out the sun.

Chameleons can change their skin colour to hide themselves (camouflage) – but they also change colour according to mood. Some go grey when depressed.

Head lice suck blood for about 45 seconds every 2–3 hours, but they can go without a meal for up to two days if they are between heads – on a comb, towel or pillow.

Geckos have transparent eyelids which are permanently closed but allow the gecko to see anyway.

A kind of yellow-bellied toad can produce a nasty foam that smells of garlic to deter attackers.

Komodo dragons are lizards 3 metres (10 feet) long. They aren't poisonous, but there are so many bacteria in their mouths – growing in rotten meat between their teeth – that a bite from one often leads to blood poisoning and death.

The naked mole rat is perhaps the ugliest mammal in the world. It looks like a wrinkly sausage with very short legs and huge, protruding teeth. It has no hair anywhere except the inside of its mouth.

The bluebottle and greenbottle flies common in houses lay their eggs in rotting meat, dead animals and animal faeces.

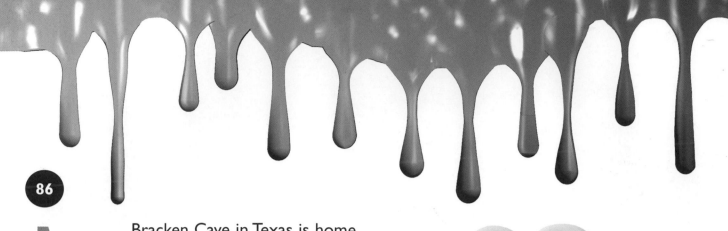

Bracken Cave in Texas is home to 20 million bats. The floor is caked in a thick layer of bat faeces.

Only female mosquitoes bite and suck blood – they need the protein in blood so that they can lay eggs. The males only eat nectar from flowers.

Crows are one of the few larger creatures that will eat rotting and putrid flesh.

A maggot doesn't have teeth – it oozes a kind of spit called *ferment* onto its food. This dissolves the food, and the maggot then sucks it up.

A hissing cockroach makes a noise by squeezing air out of tiny holes in its body segments. The sound can be heard 3.7 metres (12 feet) away.

The axolotl is a pale amphibian that is part way between a tadpole and a lizard, and lives in a single lake in Mexico. Some axolotls change shape and become land creatures, but most don't ever change.

Baby Komodo dragons will eat their brothers and sisters if they are hungry and there is no other food.

If an octopus loses a tentacle it can grow a new one.

An octopus tentacle will carry on wriggling for some time after being cut off.

A sting-ray has a special cap on the end of its tail which breaks off when it stings, allowing poison to pour out into the wound it's made in its victim.

Bat faeces lies so deep on the floors of their caves that people harvest it to sell as fertilizer for plants.

The aye-aye is a nocturnal mammal from Madagascar that has one very long, bony finger on one hand. It looks so frightening that local people believed contact with an aye-aye led to death, so they killed most of them.

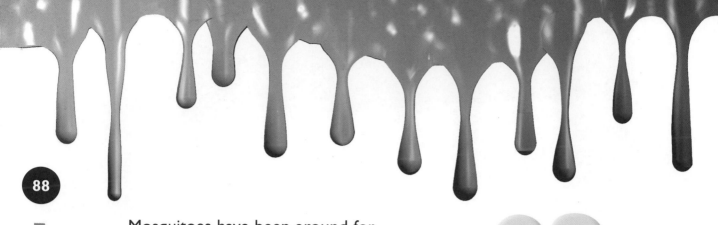

Mosquitoes have been around for 200 million years. That's so long that even dinosaurs could have been bitten by them!

Flies beat their wings about 180 times a second.

The guanay cormorant makes its nest from dried faeces.

The angler fish has a glowing blob attached to a spike at the front of its head. In the dark, deep sea the glowing blob attracts small prey which the angler fish then sucks in and gobbles up.

Electric eels can deliver a shock of 500 volts to stun their dinner into submission.

Flies eat by vomiting up something they've eaten previously so that the chemicals in their vomit can start to dissolve the new meal. When it's sloppy, they suck it all up again. That's why it's a really bad idea to eat anything a fly's been sitting on!

Sharks have special organs in their snouts and elsewhere that let them detect the electric fields produced by living animals. They can then home in on the animals to eat them.

The face fly feeds on the mucus produced in a cow's eyes and nostrils.

Plagues of flying foxes (fruit bats) can destroy a fruit orchard in a single night.

A giraffe has special valves in its arteries so that its blood can reach up to its head. Without them, it would need a heart as big as its whole body!

Land leeches in Asia can drop from trees onto people and suck out so much blood the person dies.

A cockroach can withstand more than 120 times the force of the Earth's gravity – an astronaut passes out at 12 times the pressure of gravity.

Slugs are attracted to beer; some gardeners trap them by putting out bowls of beer which the slugs fall into. They get drunk and drown. The slugs, not the gardeners!

A 32-kilogram (70-pound) octopus can squeeze through a hole the size of a tennis ball.

Goliath bird-eating spiders can grow to the size of a dinner plate and kill small birds.

The end of a chameleon's tongue can have a club-like lump oiled with sticky goo which helps it to catch insects.

The Australian blue-ringed octopus can pump out a poison that will paralyze or kill a human.

When there's not much food around, cockroaches will eat each other – ripping open the victim's stomach and tearing out the insides.

Some toads can swallow shrews and mice whole.

A head louse can lay 200–300 eggs during its life of around thirty days. The eggs only take five to ten days to hatch and start feeding.

Over 100 million years ago, crocodiles were twice the size they are now – up to 12 metres (40 feet) long – and could eat dinosaurs.

Baby cockroaches feed on their parents' faeces to get the bacteria they need to help them digest plants and vegetables.

Geckos and centipedes both eat cockroaches.

A full-grown python can swallow a pig whole.

The deadly box jellyfish that lives off the coast of Australia is the size of a basketball but has tentacles that trail 4.5 metres (15 feet). If the tentacles touch you, tiny harpoons inject poison.

If a lizard loses its tail, it can grow a new one.

A patch of rainforest soil around the size of this book can hatch 10,000 mosquito eggs.

Rabbits partially digest the grass they eat and then excrete it as soft, gluey pellets. They then eat these to finish digesting their meal properly.

Crocodiles carry their young around in their mouths.

The geographic tree frog can change its eyes from brown to patterned to help it camouflage itself in trees.

When a viper fish wants to eat a large meal, it moves all its internal organs towards its tail to make more room inside it for food.

Light-coloured spots on surfaces of food show a fly has vomited something up and tasted the surface; dark-coloured spots are fly faeces.

An elephant produces 23 kilograms (50 pounds) of faeces every day.

Vampire bats drink half their body weight in blood every day.

Cat urine glows in the dark (but it has to be very dark, if you're thinking of testing it).

A ribbon worm can eat 95 percent of its own body and still survive.

A cockroach can live for a week after its head is cut off.

When a fish called the Pacific grenadier is pulled out of the sea by fishermen, the change in pressure makes gas inside it expand quickly and its stomach pops out of its mouth.

Dogs in New York, USA, produce 18 million kilograms (40 million pounds) of faeces a year. Luckily, New Yorkers have to clear up after their dogs.

A leech will suck blood until it is ten times its original size and can't hold any more. Once it's full, it drops off its victim.

A vampire finch in the Galapagos Islands pecks holes in other birds to feed on their blood.

Leeches don't only suck from the outside of your body. If you drink water with a leech in, it can attach to the inside of your mouth or throat and, in a river, leeches can go into your bottom and suck you from the inside.

The gavial, a kind of crocodile from India, has over a hundred teeth.

The potato beetle larva protects itself from birds that want to eat it by covering itself in its own poisonous faeces.

The turkey vulture excretes faeces onto its legs to keep them cool.

The female black widow spider eats the male after mating, sometimes eating up to twenty-five partners a day. Now *that's* a man-eater!

A chameleon's tongue can be twice as long as its body, and must be kept curled to fit inside it.

A baby robin eats 4 metres (14 feet) of earthworms a day!

When a toad is sick, it vomits up its own stomach, which hangs out of its mouth for a short time before it swallows it back down.

Some leeches have three mouths, with up to a hundred teeth.

Many leeches produce a pain-killer so that you don't notice you have been bitten unless you actually see the leech.

The queen naked mole rat is the only one to have babies. She keeps the others sterile (incapable of having babies) using a special chemical in her urine.

A very stressed octopus will sometimes eat itself.

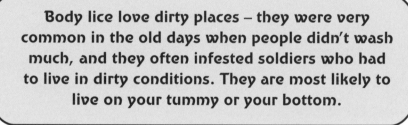

Body lice love dirty places – they were very common in the old days when people didn't wash much, and they often infested soldiers who had to live in dirty conditions. They are most likely to live on your tummy or your bottom.

A female German cockroach can produce 500,000 young in a year.

Crocodiles can't bite and chew. Instead, they hold their prey under water to drown it, then twist their bodies around to tear chunks off the victim.

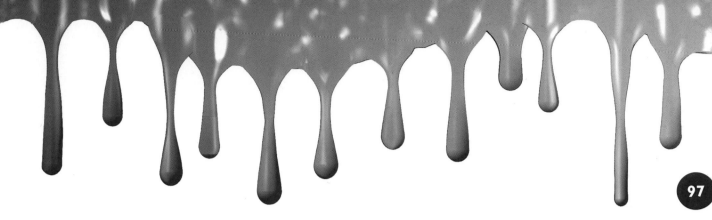

In some types of angler fish, the male is much smaller than the female and attaches himself to her body for life. After a while, he becomes fused to her and their body systems combine. His only role is to fertilize her eggs, and he is nourished by her blood.

Vultures gorging themselves on a carcass sometimes eat so much they can't fly. They then vomit to make themselves lighter.

> **Vampire bats urinate the whole time they're sucking blood. This ensures they don't get so full of blood they're too heavy to fly. So, smarter than a vulture, then!**

A dustbin can produce 30,000 flies a week from eggs laid in the rotting rubbish it contains.

> **The slime eel or hagfish feeds on dead and dying fish at the bottom of the sea. It goes into its victim through the mouth or eye socket and eats it away from the inside, leaving only a bag of skin and bones.**

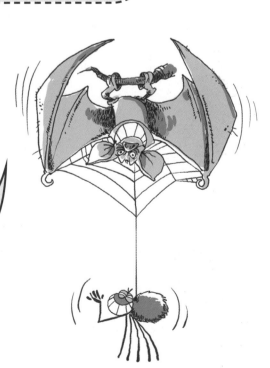

A single bat can eat 3,000–7,000 mosquitoes in a single night; a colony of 500 bats gets through a quarter of a million bugs an hour.

You could get bitten by a crocodile, but alligators don't like the taste of people.

Scorpions paralyze their prey before they suck the juices out. It's not dead, but it can't escape.

The female praying mantis begins to eat the male during mating; he carries on, but she eventually eats all of him.

When the *necrophorus* beetle finds a small dead animal, it pushes it into a suitable place, takes some of its fur to make a nest and lays its eggs near the body. When the eggs hatch into maggots, they feed on the dead body.

Bird parents eat food for their babies, fly back to the nest and vomit up the meal into the babies' open beaks.

A chicken once lived ten days after a French farmer cut its head off. He fed it with a dripper, directly into its throat.

Vampire bats don't suck – they make a cut in their victim, then lick the blood as it flows out. To keep it flowing, they have an *anticoagulant* in their spit – a chemical which stops blood from clotting and forming a scab.

Some types of octopus contain a poison which instantly kills anything that eats it.

The Pharaoh ant likes to live in hospitals where it feasts on wounds, bloody bandages and solutions for dripping into patient's bodies.

African dung beetles eat animal faeces. Five thousand beetles can eat a pound of faeces in 2 hours.

A single female fly can hatch up to 1,000 babies (maggots) in her lifetime.

A giraffe can lick inside its own ears.

A lamprey is like an eel but has no jaws. Instead, it has a sucker-like mouth with rows of teeth. It attaches itself to a fish, digs itself in and then sucks all the fluids out of the fish, eventually killing it.

Head lice have two sharp mouth parts – one cuts through your skin and sucks up blood, the other pumps out spit containing a chemical that stops your blood clotting.

Soldier flies like to lay their eggs in human faeces. The larvae (maggots) are often found in bathrooms as they crawl up the sewage pipes.

Cockroaches breed so fast that if all the young survived and reproduced, there would be 10 million cockroaches from a single pair by the end of a year.

A shark will eat parts of its own body that have been cut off or bitten off by another animal.

Some types of baby Australian spider bite limbs off their mother to feed on over several weeks.

Scorpions can withstand extremes of temperature and even radiation. A scorpion could be frozen in a block of ice for three weeks and walk away unharmed, and survive 200 times the dose of radiation that would kill a person!

Some leeches can suck enough blood in one meal to keep them alive for nine months.

Horn flies attack bulls – as many as 10,000 can land on a bull's back and suck its blood until it dies.

Locusts, like giant grasshoppers or crickets, travel in swarms of up to 80 million and each eats its own weight in plants every day.

The Japanese beetle found in Canada and the USA can eat through a human eardrum.

Cows partly digest the grass they eat, then vomit it back up into their mouths and chew and swallow it all over again. That's what they're doing when you see them chewing in a field when they're not munching on a fresh mouthful of grass.

The female hissing cockroach surrounds her eggs with a frothy substance that hardens; she then carries them inside her body for two weeks until they hatch.

If one vampire bat is too ill to leave the cave, another will suck blood all night then come home and vomit it up over the poorly bat so it doesn't miss out on a meal.

The rattle on a rattlesnake's tail is made of rings of dead skin. It builds up as the snake grows older, so the louder the rattle the larger the snake.

The butcher bird (shrike) impales mice, small birds and lizards onto spikes to hold them still while it eats them.

An elephant's trunk is so handy that it can pluck a single blade of grass from the ground.

A jellyfish excretes faeces through its mouth – it has only one opening and uses it for all purposes.

South American cane toads have special glands behind their eyes which ooze poison out of their skin. They can even shoot the poison up to 30 centimetres (nearly a foot) to deter animals that might want to eat them.

Cockroaches have an oily coating to make them slithery.

If you're attacked by a moray eel, the only way to get it off is to kill it, cut the head off and break the jaws. It won't let go while it's alive.

There are over 3,000 different types of mosquito and they live all over the world, even in the coldest places near the North and South Poles.

Aardvarks and anteaters enjoy nothing better than slurping up ants and termites with their long, sticky tongues.

Driver ants and army ants both march in massive colonies and will strip to the bones any animal they come across. They'll even tackle a wounded crocodile or lion that can't get away. Driver ants slash at their victims who eventually bleed to death from thousands of tiny cuts.

Flies have 1,500 tiny taste hairs on their feet so that they can taste what they are standing on.

Inuit people have to cover all exposed skin with a thick layer of mud to avoid fierce biting flies in the summer.

A starfish can turn its stomach inside out, pushing it out through its mouth opening.

You can cut a leech in half while it is feeding and it will carry on sucking, the blood spurting out of the cut end of its body.

Fossilized cockroaches 300 million years old have been found. This means they were around 100 million years before the dinosaurs evolved!

A flea can jump up to 220 times its own body length – a flea the size of an adult human could jump over a 25-storey building and more than a 0.4 kilometre (quarter of a mile) along the ground.

The armadillo produces so much spit that it has a special reservoir to store it in.

A grotesque frog which can turn from green to beige often lives in letterboxes and toilet cisterns in Australia and New Guinea.

Rats that hibernate together sometimes get their tails tied up in a knot. If they urinate over themselves in the winter, they can freeze together in a block. A knot of rats is called a king rat.

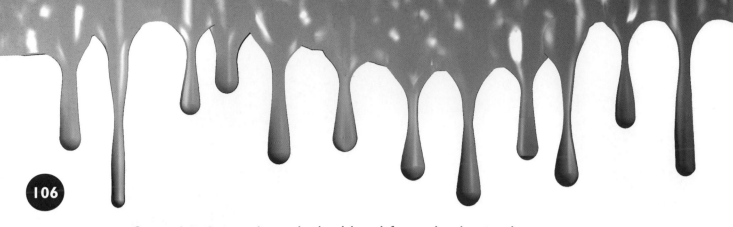

Some leeches only suck the blood from dead animals.

When a turtle (which is immune to jellyfish stings) eats a Portuguese man-of-war jellyfish, it produces a smell that attracts sharks – so the jellyfish eventually gets its revenge!

Eye gnats are attracted to the moisture produced by your eyes and nose. In the USA, they are a common nuisance on hot summer evenings. They lay their eggs in rotting vegetable matter or animal faeces.

Termites fart out between 20 and 80 million tons of gas every year (not each, all together).

Flea larvae eat their parents' faeces – or each other.

The African clawed toad lays up to 10,000 eggs, but many of its tadpoles are deformed. The parents eat the deformed ones when they hatch.

Scorpions sometimes eat their own babies.

The horned lizard from South America shoots blood out of its eyes when it is attacked. It increases the blood pressure in its sinuses until they explode, spraying blood onto the attacker.

The slime eel or hagfish produces slimy mucus from pores in its body. If something disturbs it, it throws out strings of mucus which makes the sea around it jelly-like, gunky and impossible to swim through. They can suffocate on their own slime if they over-do it.

Octopi sometimes remove stinging tentacles from jellyfish and use them as weapons.

A praying mantis is an insect rather like a cricket, but up to 12 centimetres (5 inches) long. It can kill and eat small lizards and birds, holding them impaled on a special spike it has developed for the purpose. A really hungry mantis will eat its own babies.

Cockroaches can make themselves super-slim, and can flatten their bodies to a size just a little thicker than a piece of paper to crawl into cracks.

When an opossum is threatened, it plays dead – it lies still, its tongue hanging out, excretes faeces on itself and oozes green slime that smells of rotting flesh.

A flea can jump 30,000 times without stopping.

When a large batch of mosquito eggs hatches all at once, the babies might all attack the same unfortunate animal wandering past. They can suck it dry and kill it, if it's a small animal and there are enough mosquitoes.

The babies of the Surinam toad grow under the mother's skin on her back. They stay there for up to 130 days.

The echidna is a mammal which lays an egg and keeps it in a pouch on its stomach.

The pouch grows just before the female produces the egg and disappears again after the baby has left it.

The eyes of a chameleon can move separately, so it can look in two directions at once.

The deep-sea angler fish can stretch its stomach to swallow prey much larger than itself.

Some types of botflies lay their eggs on the abdomen of another blood-sucking insect such as a flea or tick. The eggs hatch while the host feeds the larvae and burrows into the skin of the animal it's sucking on.

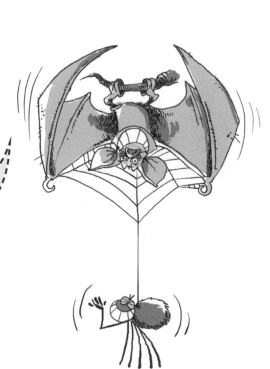

Three-toed sloths move so slowly that algae often grows on their fur.

Newly discovered monster of the deep, Dakosaurus, was 4 metres (almost 14 feet) long, and had a head like a meat-eating dinosaur but the flippers and tail of a fish. Luckily, it died out 135 million years ago!

The embryos of tiger sharks fight each other in the womb, the strongest killing and eating the others so that only one is ever born.

If a barracuda fish falls ill, it eats things that will make its flesh poisonous. That way, anything that eats it after it dies will be poisoned.

Horrible History Facts

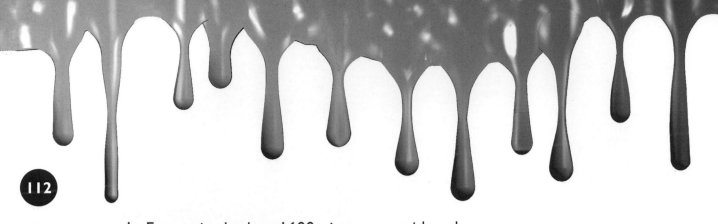

In France in the late 1600s, it was considered a great honour to talk to King Louis XIV while he was on the lavatory.

In Anglo-Saxon times, shepherds were given twelve days' worth of cow manure at Christmas.

Vikings used rancid butter to style and dress their hair.

Biological warfare has been used since 600 BCE when the Greek city Cirrha was besieged by Solon. He poisoned the water supply with hellebore roots and stormed the city while the citizens had diarrhoea.

During the 900 days of the siege of Leningrad in the Second World War, 1,500 people were accused of cannibalism.

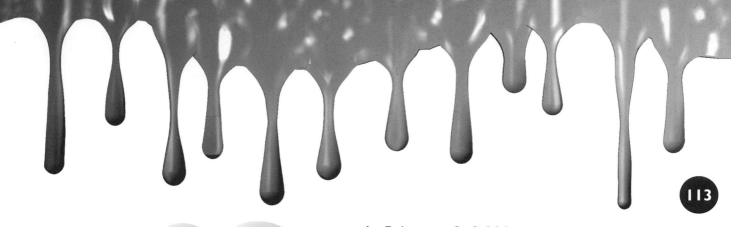

In Palestine 8–9,000 years ago, a dead relative was buried under the floor of the family's house – except the head. The flesh and brain were removed from the head and the skull used as the base for a plaster mould of the person's head, which was decorated and kept.

The Greeks played the game knucklebones with real bones from the knuckles of animals that have cloven feet – like pigs, goats and antelopes.

After a massacre carried out by Indian soldiers in 1857, the British soldiers made the Indians clean up the blood – and those who refused had to lick it up.

Slaves sometimes had to fight to the death in a Roman arena. To make sure they weren't just pretending to be dead, they could be prodded with a red-hot poker and hit on the head with a huge hammer.

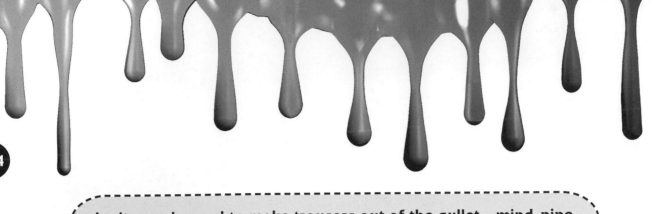

Inuit people used to make trousers out of the gullet – wind-pipe – of a seal or walrus, using one for each leg.

Theban king Mithradites (132–63 BCE) took small doses of poison regularly to develop immunity and protect himself from poisoners. When he later wanted to kill himself, the poison he took did not kill him.

Wig-makers suffered during times of plague as people thought the disease could be caught from wigs made of human hair. So many second-hand wigs were infested with fleas that they were probably right!

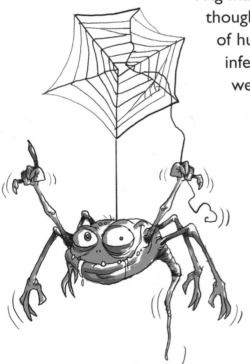

In Sparta, Greece, in 600 BCE the law required that a child born imperfect – disabled or deformed – be killed immediately.

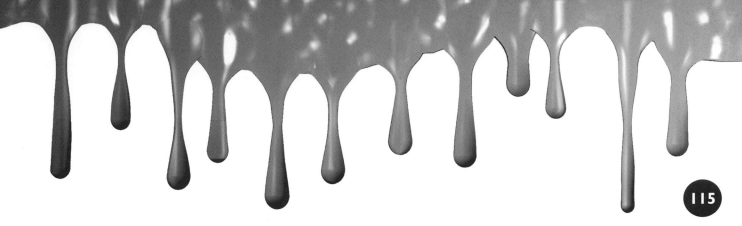

Toad-eaters were people employed by men selling medicine at fairs and markets. The toad-eater had to swallow a toad – supposed to be deadly poisonous – and then take the medicine. Their survival encouraged people to buy the medicine. They may or may not have actually swallowed the toads…

Victorian child chimney sweeps sometimes had to crawl through chimneys as narrow as 18 centimetres (7 inches). If they didn't go quickly enough, their bare feet were pricked with burning straws.

Birching was allowed as a punishment in Britain until the 1940s. It consisted of being beaten on the bare buttocks with a bunch of twigs.

In Ancient Egypt, women kept a cone of grease on their head. During the day, it melted in the hot sun and dripped down, making their hair gleam with grease.

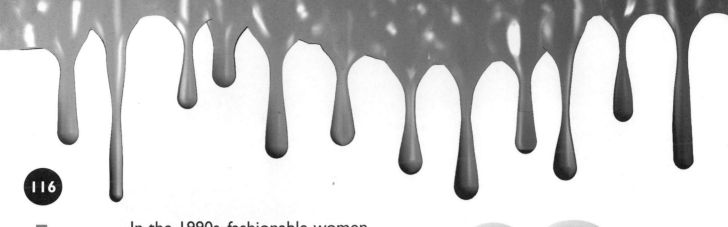

In the 1990s, fashionable women in Europe who wanted to look thin wore corsets laced so tightly that their ribs were sometimes broken!

During the Great Plague that struck England in 1665–66, boys at Eton school were punished for not smoking – smoking was thought to protect them from the disease.

In the nineteenth century, a school headmaster in York, England, massacred his pupils and hid their bodies in cupboards.

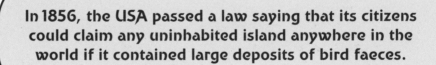

In 1856, the USA passed a law saying that its citizens could claim any uninhabited island anywhere in the world if it contained large deposits of bird faeces.

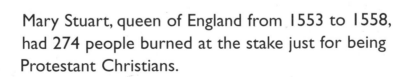

Mary Stuart, queen of England from 1553 to 1558, had 274 people burned at the stake just for being Protestant Christians.

Before written or computerized records helped us to keep track of criminals, many countries marked criminals with a tattoo or a branding iron – a red hot iron used to burn a pattern, letter or picture into their skin. This meant that everyone could see what they had done.

Pope Clement VII tried eating a death cap toadstool in 1534; it killed him.

Bird faeces called *guano* were collected and sold from Peru, Chile and Bolivia for hundreds of years. It was used as a fertilizer for plants.

A common way of attacking a besieged castle or city in the Middle Ages was to catapult dead animals, corpses or even the heads of enemies over the walls.

The Greek emperor Draco died when he was smothered by the hats and cloaks that admirers threw over him at a party.

It took over two months to make an Egyptian mummy. After removing the internal organs and brain, the body was covered with a kind of salt for two months to dry out, then treated with resin, packed with sand and sawdust and wrapped in bandages.

Mongol leader Tamerlane the Great (1336–1405) executed anyone who told him a joke he had already heard.

In 2,350 BC the Mesopotamian king Urukagina demanded that thieves be stoned to death with stones carved with their crime.

Roman prisoners condemned to fight to death with each other or wild animals often tried to kill themselves before the fight. One man pushed a wooden spike down his throat – it was used for holding the sponge people cleaned themselves with in the lavatory.

Anglo-Saxon peasants sometimes wove clothes made out of dried stinging nettles.

Anyone who rebelled against the Mesopotamian king Ashurnasirpal could expect to be skinned or buried alive. We know this because he buried some rebels inside a column and carved the story of their crime on the outside.

In Ancient Rome, vestal virgins were young girls who served in a temple and could not be touched. If they committed a crime their punishment was to be buried alive as it could be done without anyone touching them.

The Romans had criminals torn apart by wild animals while the public watched. Dogs or lions were usually used, but sometimes more exotic animals were brought in.

In the time of King Charles II of England, who reigned from 1649 to 1685, dead people had to buried in a shroud made of wool, to boost business for the wool trade.

In Anglo-Saxon England, people who died in a famine were eaten by their neighbours!

The scarab beetle was treated as holy by the Ancient Egyptians. Scarab beetles roll themselves in a ball of faeces and lay their eggs in it.

The Roman king Tarquin crucified anyone who committed suicide – even though they were already dead – to show other people what would happen to their bodies if they did the same.

In 1740, a cow found guilty of witchcraft was hanged.

A medieval trial of guilt required a suspected criminal to plunge their hand into a pan of hot water and take out a stone, or carry a red-hot iron bar. The injured arm was bandaged and inspected after three days. If it was healed the person was considered innocent. If not, they were guilty and were punished.

In 167 BCE, a Roman commander had a group of soldiers trampled to death by elephants for deserting (running away from battle).

The Mongolian ruler Ghengis Khan imposed the death penalty for urinating in water because water was so precious in the Mongolian desert.

The Spanish Inquisition was set up to find people who committed crimes against the church and its teachings. They often questioned and tortured people until they confessed. In the case of a child under 10, though, they could go straight to the torture and not bother with the questions.

Lord Nelson (1758–1805) admiral of the English fleet, slept in a coffin in his cabin. The coffin was made from the mast of an enemy French ship.

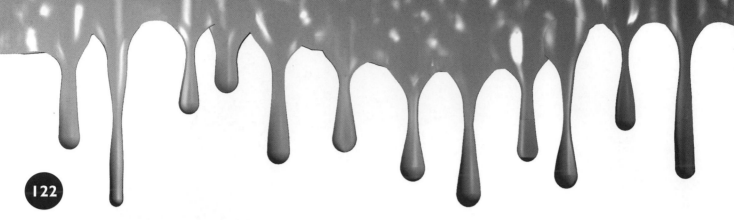

During the time of Henry VIII of England, who reigned from 1508 to 1547, the punishment for poisoners was to be boiled alive.

To make violin strings, the gut of a sheep – which could be 30 metres long (over 98 feet) in length – was removed intact. The blood, flesh and fat were then scraped off the outside, the half-digested grass was squeezed out and it was washed out carefully. The wider end was used as sausage skins, the rest for violin strings.

In India, people used to believe that the eyes from a slow lorris – a nocturnal creature like a monkey with no tail – could work as a love potion.

An Ancient Egyptian cure for burns involved warming a frog in goat dung and applying it to the burn.

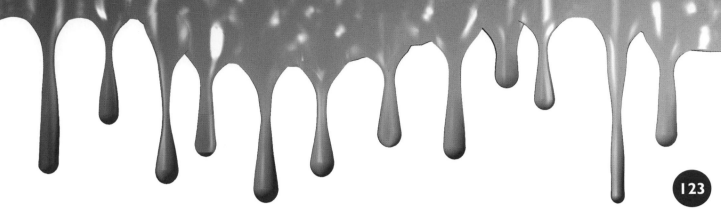

The Roman emperor Valerian was captured by visigoths (a barbaric tribe) invading Rome in 260 CE, who skinned him alive and then displayed the skin as a signal of their triumph.

When Sir Walter Ralegh was executed in 1618, his wife had his head embalmed. She carried it around with her for 29 years, until her own death.

Ancient Greeks used to blow up a pig's bladder like a balloon and use it as a ball.

An Anglo-Saxon cure for baldness was to rub the ash from burnt bees into the head.

Soldiers fighting in the trenches in World War I often suffered from trench foot (spending too long in cold, wet trenches made their feet rot). Some had to have their feet amputated because of it...

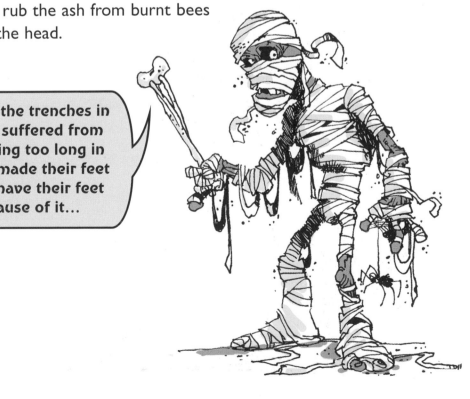

A French medieval torture involved trapping a person in the stocks – a wooden structure that held their ankles while they sat on the ground – pouring salt water over their bare feet and letting a goat lick it off.

The Hungarian countess Elizabeth Bathori killed more than 600 young girls in the 1500s in order to drink and bathe in their blood.

The servants of a dead Egyptian pharaoh were often killed and buried with him or sealed alive in his pyramid.

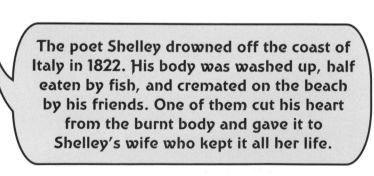

The poet Shelley drowned off the coast of Italy in 1822. His body was washed up, half eaten by fish, and cremated on the beach by his friends. One of them cut his heart from the burnt body and gave it to Shelley's wife who kept it all her life.

Hanging, drawing and quartering was a punishment for the worst crimes in England from 1241. The prisoner was nearly strangled by hanging, then cut open and had his innards removed and cooked in front of him, and finally chopped into four pieces. By the mid-1700s, prisoners were killed before the drawing and quartering.

Monks in Sicily, Italy, mummified dead bodies until 1920. A display of 6,000 can be seen in catacombs in Palermo, standing around or lying on shelves.

A Saxon cure for madness was a beating with a whip made from the skin of a dolphin.

Ancient Egyptians sometimes brought a mummified body to banquets to remind diners that one day they would die.

Early Colonists in America used to clean their windows with rags dipped in urine.

In the Middle Ages, butchers often killed animals for meat in their shops, then threw the innards out into the street.

Fashionable women in Japan and Vietnam stained their teeth black until the mid-1900s.

Romans who killed a relative would be executed by being tied in a sack with a live dog, cockerel, snake and monkey and thrown into a river.

Wool used to be softened by people trampling on it in a large vat of stale (two-week-old) urine and ground clay. The people who did this were called 'fullers'.

During a famine and drought in Jamestown, America, in 1609, one settler was executed for eating his dead wife.

A dead body found in the Alps in 1991 was at first thought to be a climber who had died. Investigators discovered it was a man who had been mummified naturally in the ice after dying 5,300 years ago. They named him Otzi.

So many people associated with the discovery of Otzi have died young that some believe the mummy is cursed.

The Incas of South America used to mummify their dead kings and leave them sitting on their thrones.

People hunting animals examine the faeces of their quarry to find out information about the size, sex and type of animal. In the Middle Ages, hunters often carried the faeces around with them while they hunted, storing them in their hunting horn.

Queen Christina of Sweden, who reigned from 1640 to 1654, had a miniature cannon and crossbow for executing fleas.

The French actress Sarah Bernhardt took a coffin with her on all her travels. She learned her lines while lying in the coffin and even entertained her lovers in it.

In the 1700s, people wore huge hairstyles made of a mixture of real hair and horse hair or other fibres. As they rarely cleaned them – keeping them in place for months on end – they carried sticks to knock vermin out of their hair-does.

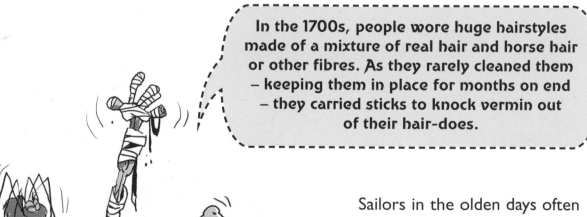

Sailors in the olden days often had a single gold tooth, which could be pulled out and used to pay for their funeral if they died away from home.

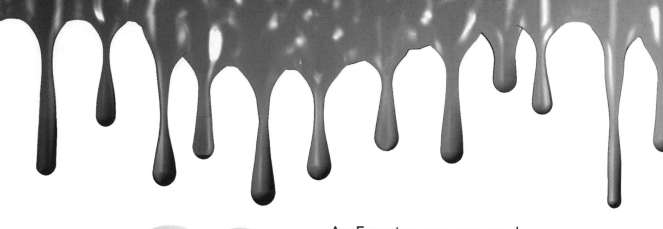

An Egyptian mummy can have more than 20 layers of bandages, with glue between the layers. Every finger and toe was wrapped separately. It took 15 days to wrap a royal mummy.

In the 1700s, European women had their gums pierced so that they could fit hooks to hold their false teeth in place.

Ancient Romans made hair dye from pigeon faeces.

Uruguay's rugby team was stranded in the Andes in South America after a plane crash in 1979. It took seventy days for them to be rescued, and they had to eat the other passengers who had died in the crash.

An Ancient Egyptian who was feeling a bit unwell might eat a mixture of mashed mouse and faeces. Mmmmmmm, bound to make you feel better!

In 1846, eighty-seven pioneers crossing the mountains of Nevada, USA, became trapped in bad weather. By the end of the winter, forty of them had been eaten by the others.

King Pepi II of Egypt had himself surrounded by naked slaves smeared with honey so that any biting flies would be attracted to them and not bite him.

In the 1800s, flea circuses were popular – the fleas were glued into costumes and stuck to wires or each other to look as though they were performing tricks.

Mongolian leader Tamerlane played polo using the skulls of enemies killed in battle.

Ivan the Terrible blinded the two architects who designed his new church of Saint Basil's so that they could never make anything more beautiful.

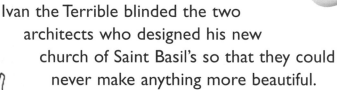

The Russian ruler Peter the Great had his wife's lover decapitated and insisted that she keep his head in a jar of alcohol beside her bed as a reminder of her crime.

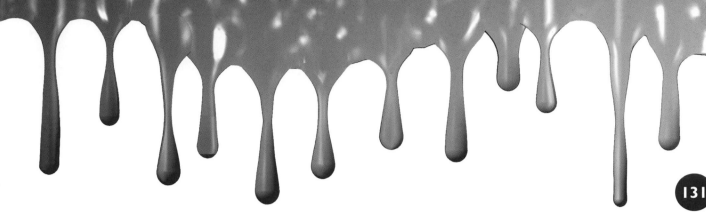

In China in the 1500s, a common method of committing suicide was by eating a pound of salt.

Vlad the Impaler, ruler of Transylvania, had over 20,000 enemies impaled on spikes between 1456 and 1476.

The word 'thug' comes from 'Thuggees', who were an Indian cult — sometimes described as the world's first mafia — who used to trick and murder people as human sacrifices to their goddess Kali.

In the 1600s and later, Egyptian mummies were ground up to use in medicines around Europe.

In the Middle Ages, people made washing powder from wood ash and urine.

In the 1700s, fashionable European women commonly shaved off their real eyebrows and stuck on false ones made from mouse fur.

A Bohemian army general was so devoted to his country that when he died he asked for his skin to be removed and made into a drum that could be beaten in defiance of Bohemia's enemies. It was used nearly 200 years later at the start of the Thirty Years War in 1618.

British king James I's tongue was too large for his mouth so he slobbered all the time and was a very messy eater.

Charles I was executed by beheading, but had his head sewn back on so that his family could pay their respects to his body. His doctor stole a bone from his neck and had it made into a salt cellar.

In 1981,
300 people
thrown into the
water in a ferry
accident in Brazil
were eaten alive
by piranha.

London prisoners condemned
to death used to go to chapel
on the Sunday before their
execution where they had
to sit around a coffin
while the priest told them
how sinful they were.

In times of famine, Stone
Age tribes would eat old
women before dogs – they
thought them less useful.

The body tag from the corpse of Lee Harvey Oswald,
who shot President John F. Kennedy, was sold for
£3,600 at an auction.

James, Duke of Monmouth, was beheaded in 1685
but when it was discovered that there was no official
portrait of him, his head was stitched back on and he
posed for his portrait at last.

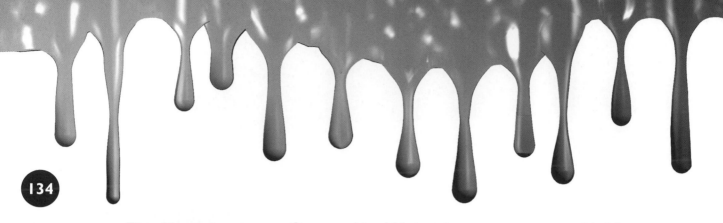

The fifteenth-century German king Wenceslas was so angry with his chef after a particularly bad meal that he had him roasted alive.

Saint Ignatius of Antioch prayed to be eaten by wild animals; when the Roman Emperor Trajan sentenced him to be eaten by lions in 110 CE he fell to his knees and thanked him.

In 896, the rotting body of Pope Formosus was removed from his coffin, dressed in his papal robes and put on trial. Found guilty, his blessing finger was cut off and he was thrown in the river.

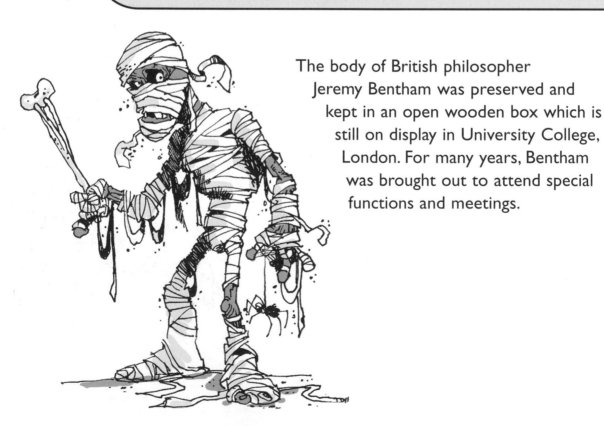

The body of British philosopher Jeremy Bentham was preserved and kept in an open wooden box which is still on display in University College, London. For many years, Bentham was brought out to attend special functions and meetings.

Russian leader Peter the Great had a museum in which he kept the stuffed bodies of deformed people and animals, such as a child with two heads and a sheep with five feet. The museum was looked after by a deformed dwarf who knew he would become an exhibit when he died.

It took the executioner three blows to behead Mary Queen of Scots in 1567. And he still had to saw through the remaining skin and gristle with a knife.

Roman gladiator and slave rebel leader Spartacus had 300 of his followers crucified to show the others what would happen to them if they deserted his army.

During the Reign of Terror following the French Revolution, 17,000 people were beheaded using the guillotine.

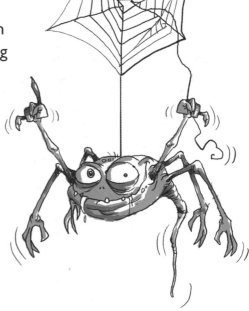

The Scottish bagpipes were originally made from the entire skin or stomach of a dead sheep.

In Ancient Egypt, a flea-catcher would cover himself in milk and stand in the middle of the flea-infested room until all the fleas jumped onto him then he'd leave, taking them all with him.

English hatmakers used to soften the straw they plaited into hats by spitting on it.

King Kokodo of the Congo ruled for three years after his death. His body was wheeled around in a box during this part of his reign…

In the 1800s, there were several cases of people being buried when not really dead. Terrible stories about opened coffins with scratch marks on the inside, and corpses with fingernails worn away by trying to escape, led to cautious people being buried with a system of warning bells fitted in the coffin which they could ring if they woke up.

During witchcraft trials in Salem, Massachusetts, USA, in 1692, 25 people were condemned to death on the flimsy evidence of a group of hysterical girls.

It is said that the cursed mummy of Egyptian princess Amen-Ra was on board the Titanic when it sank in 1912, killing 1,500 people. The mummy was being sent from the British Museum to the USA; only the lid of the mummy's coffin is still in the British Museum.

Ivan the Terrible of Russia punished a bishop by having him stitched into the skin of a dead bear and releasing a pack of hounds to hunt and kill him.

Bald Romans used to make a paste of mashed up flies and spread it over their heads in the belief that it would make their hair regrow. It didn't...

Instead of a hollow pumpkin with a candle inside, Celtic people are said to have used real human heads cut from defeated enemies to keep away ghosts and ghouls in the autumn.

Leather used to be cured with a mixture of dog and chicken faeces smeared on it for many months. The fat and rotting meat scraps were scraped off with a knife.

1001 Horrible Facts

In the past, European women sometimes wore a tube filled with sticky tree sap around their necks or on animal fur. These were supposed to attract and trap any fleas on their bodies.

The earliest cosmetic surgery was practised by doctors in India who made fake noses for criminals who had their noses cut off as a punishment for their crimes.

Chimney sweeps used to have three baths a year – one in the spring, one in the autumn and one for Christmas. The rest of the time, they were covered in soot.

If sheep grazed on pastures full of clover, shepherds sometimes had to puncture the stomachs of sheep with a sharp knife to release all the gases that built up inside them.

In the Middle Ages a royal farter was employed to jump around farting in front of the king to amuse him.

In the old days, a 'whipping boy' used to sit next to a royal prince in lessons. If the prince made a mistake, or did something wrong, the whipping boy was punished instead of the prince.

In Africa, it was common to bend back springy saplings and tie them beneath the ears of someone about to be beheaded, so that the person's last sensation would be of their head flying through the air.

A common test for the guilt of a person accused of witchcraft was to throw them in a pond. If they floated, they were guilty and were executed. If they sank, they were innocent – but probably drowned.

Until 1868, criminals could be transported from England – sent to Australia for seven or fourteen years – for even petty crimes. The youngest victim was a boy of nine, transported for stealing.

King Henry VIII of England, employed the death penalty more than any other English king in history.

A punishment used in China in the old days was for a prisoner to be kept in an iron cage with his head sticking out the top. The cage was too tall to sit in, and too short to stand up. Some prisoners were left to starve to death inside.

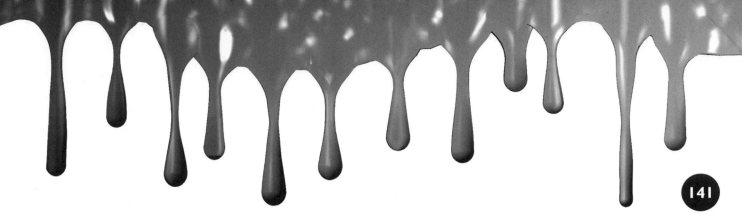

At banquets, the Gauls used to award the legs of roast animals to the bravest warriors. Sometimes fights to the death resulted from the squabbles over who should get them.

Vlad the Impaler used to entertain guests to dinner surrounded by the bodies of people he had executed, impaled on spikes.

Long ago, criminals would be hanged in a metal cage called a gibbet, or in chains, near the scene of their crime 'until their bones rotted to nothing'.

In 1577, an outbreak of typhus in an Oxford jail killed 300 people – the judges, jury, witnesses and spectators at criminal trials. The prisoners, used to living in filthy conditions, all survived.

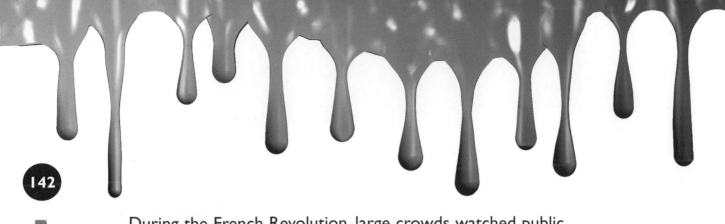

During the French Revolution, large crowds watched public executions by guillotine and people would rush forward to try to collect blood dripping from the heads lifted to show the crowd. They would keep bloody handkerchieves as souvenirs of the outing.

In 1857, a group of Indian people who rebelled against the ruling British were strapped across the mouths of live cannons and blown to bits when cannon balls were shot through them.

People who killed themselves used to be buried at a cross-roads with a stake through their heart. It was thought that they couldn't go to heaven, and the cross-roads would confuse their ghost so that it couldn't find the way home to haunt anyone.

A trusted servant of William of Orange, a Dutch king of England, spent money the king had given him for clothes on pistols, which he used to shoot the king. As punishment, he had his flesh pulled off with red-hot pincers, his guts pulled out and his body cut into pieces.

Inca women washed their hair in week-old urine, braided it, and then used more old urine to keep it in place.

The first person to be found guilty of a crime on the basis of finger print evidence was an Argentinian woman who murdered her children in 1892. Her fingerprints were found in blood on a door frame.

In Ancient Babylon, a doctor who accidentally killed a patient had his hands cut off.

A punishment for an English woman who nagged her husband or gossiped too much was to wear a metal cage over her head called a 'scold's bridle'. It had a spiked plate inside her mouth that would cut her tongue if she moved it to speak.

In 1685, a wolf that terrorized a village near Ansbach in Germany was sentenced to be dressed in human clothing and hanged.

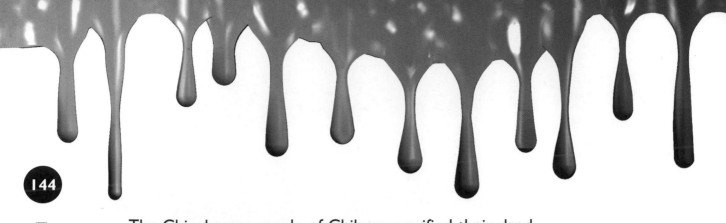

The Chinchorro people of Chile mummified their dead 8,000 years ago. They cut off the arms and legs, removed and smoked the skin, strapped sticks to the bones and replaced all the soft parts with grass and ashes, then put the whole body back together and painted it.

It is reported that during Napoleon's invasion of Russia in 1812 some soldiers cut open dead horses and sheltered inside them to avoid freezing to death.

During excavations at a circle of standing stones in Avebury, England, in 1938, archaeologists found the body of a man who had been crushed under a falling stone in the 1320s when villagers tried to bury the stones.

Over 100,000 people have been tried for witchcraft in Europe since 1100, most of them tortured and eventually executed.

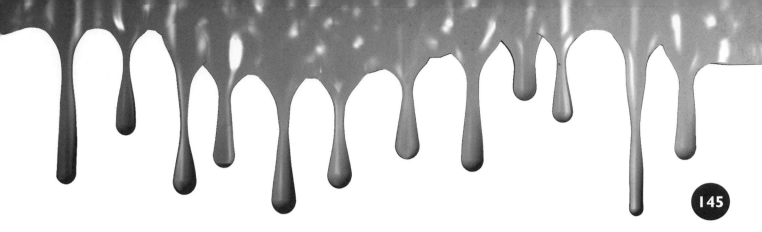

English revolutionary Oliver Cromwell died of natural causes, but opponents had his body dug up, tried and executed. His head is kept in an unmarked location in Sidney Sussex College, Cambridge.

Some Stone-Age people believed the spirit could only escape when the flesh had gone from the body, so they left corpses to rot or be eaten by wild animals, or hacked off the flesh, before burying them.

As well as people, the ancient Egyptians mummified all kinds of animals including cats, crocodiles, birds – even fish and dung beetles.

A 1,000-year-old grave in England was found to contain a rich woman in a coffin beneath a poor woman pinned down by a big stone. She was probably a slave, buried alive to serve the rich woman after death.

At the Aztec festival celebrating Xipe Totec – the Aztec god of spring – prisoners of war were flayed alive. Their skins were then worn ceremonially by priests to represent the renewal of earth and the start of new life in spring.

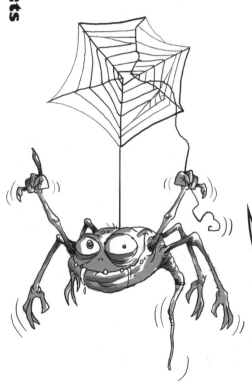

People of the North American Sioux tribe used to make an amulet of their own, dried umbilical cord – the cord which connects the unborn baby to its mother's body – which they thought guaranteed a long life.

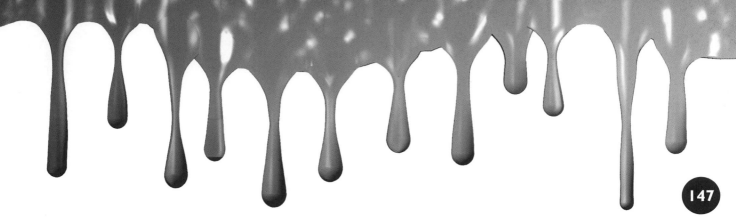

A lhasa apso dog was once imprisoned and kept on death row in a prison in Washington, USA, for over eight years for biting.

For nearly 1,000 years, Chinese women had their feet bound to keep them small. The toes were bent underneath, breaking all the bones, and the feet were kept tightly bandaged from childhood until death. The practice was banned in 1911.

The ancient Britons used to practise euthanasia by jumping off cliffs to their deaths. If individuals were too elderly to jump they would be pushed!

In the 1700s, the penalty for wearing tartan or playing the bagpipes in Britain was death.

Anglo-Saxon parents were allowed to sell children up to the age of seven to be slaves 'if they needed to do so'.

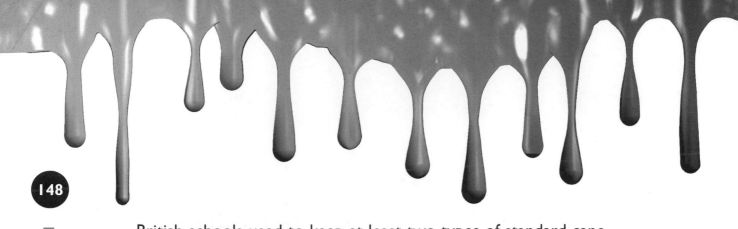

British schools used to keep at least two types of standard cane for hitting naughty children. Children over 15 years of age could be hit with the senior cane, which was longer and thicker than that used on younger children.

People used to believe that smearing their clothes with fat from a dead pig would keep away fleas.

The Jivaros in the Andes shrunk the heads of enemies killed in battle. They skinned the head, then stitched up the eyes and mouth and stewed the skin for a couple of hours with herbs. Then they dried it, stuffed it with hot stones and sand and polished it.

Apart from the heart, an Egyptian mummy doesn't have any internal organs left inside the body. The others were removed and put into separate canopic jars that were buried with it.

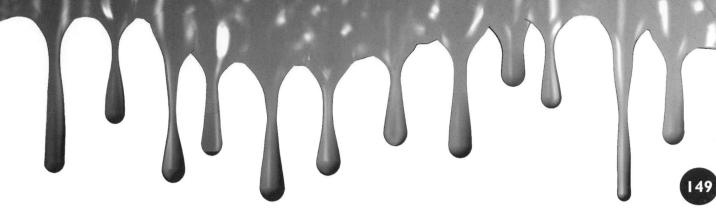

In the War of the Pacific (1879–1884), Chile fought against Bolivia and Peru over who was allowed to collect bird faeces and whether they should have to pay a tax on them.

Before modern plumbing, a gong scourer was a boy who was sent into cess pits to scoop and scrape all the muck into buckets and remove it. The job was so horrible it was done at night so that people wouldn't have to see it happening.

When King Philip of Spain died in 1560, his devastated wife would not allow him to be buried, but had his coffin accompany her everywhere.

Csar Peter III of Russia was crowned 34 years after he died. His coffin was opened so that the crown could be put on his head.

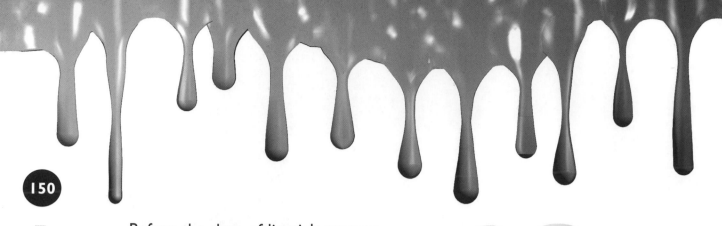

Before the days of lipstick, women used to colour their lips red with *cochineal*, a paste made from crushed beetles.

The law system drawn up by the Roman emperor Draco made every crime a capital offence – one for which the criminal could be executed.

Before the invention of real footballs, kids used to stuff a pig's bladder with peas to kick around.

The body of William the Conqueror was too big for his coffin, so two soldiers jumped up and down on him to try to squish him in. This broke his back and made his stomach explode.

In the Middle Ages, the boys who looked after dogs used for hunting had to sleep in the kennels with them.

In England, suicide used to be illegal. The punishment for trying to kill yourself was death.

Ancient Romans used to make themselves sick during a banquet so that they could eat more after they were full. A special slave had the job of clearing up the mess.

In medieval France, a cockerel that was found sitting on an egg (which only hens normally do) was found guilty of being a devil and was burned at the stake.

In 1808, Tommy Otter was hanged for killing his girlfriend. His body was left chained in a tree and a year later a pair of blue tits made a nest in his skull and reared eight chicks.

Archaeologists in Peru have found skeletons of victims tied up and left to be eaten by vultures, perhaps as a sacrifice.

To honour the goddess Teteoinnan at the time of harvest, the Aztecs skinned a woman as a sacrifice. Her skin was then worn by a priest at a harvest festival.

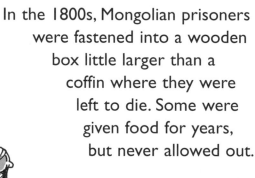

In the 1800s, Mongolian prisoners were fastened into a wooden box little larger than a coffin where they were left to die. Some were given food for years, but never allowed out.

Houses in many parts of the world have been made from a mixture called wattle and daub – horse manure and straw.

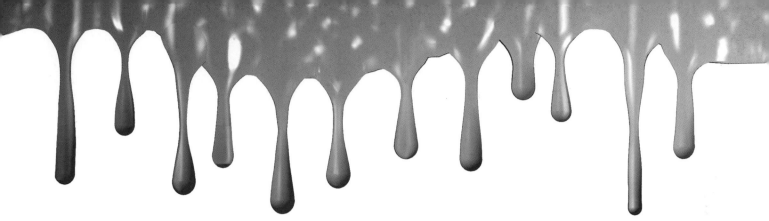

Horrible
Science Facts

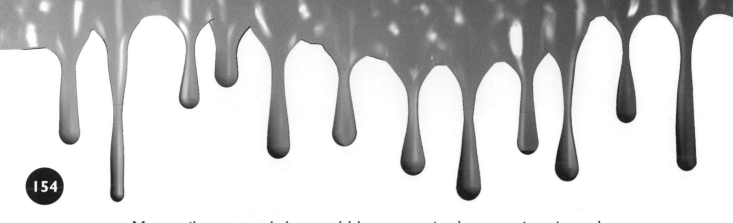

Many tribes around the world have practised trepanning since the Stone Age. It involves drilling a hole in the skull, often with a stone, to ease headaches by letting out evil spirits. People frequently survived, as many skulls have been found with several such holes, some partially healed.

In 1962, a Dutch doctor decided to try trepanning. He used an electric drill to make a hole in his own head.

Early Indian surgeons used ants to hold the edges of wounds together. They would get an ant to bite through both sides of the wound, then twist off the ant's body and throw it away, leaving the head in place with the jaws acting as a stitch.

Malaria is a deadly disease spread by mosquitoes. It is caused by a tiny parasite that lives inside a person's blood cells. Malaria kills 1–3 million people a year.

Railway workers in France in the 1800s claimed to have freed a Pterodactyl trapped in rock. They said it flapped, squawked and died. Reports of frogs and other animals trapped in solid rock are quite common, but not scientifically proven.

If you fell into a black hole you would be stretched into an incredibly long, thin string in a process called 'spaghettification'.

Snake venom is not normally poisonous if swallowed because stomach acid alters the chemicals in it.

A toxin in the nectar of laurels and rhododendrons makes honey made from these plants poisonous. In 66 BCE, Roman troops were lured by their enemies into a grove where bees made honey from these flowers. The soldiers ate it and were slaughtered while sick.

The scientific name for a fear of peanut butter sticking to the roof of your mouth is *arachibutyrophobia*.

Cells taken from the inside of baby teeth when they fall out have been grown and have reproduced in the laboratory. Put into the jaws of mice, they grow into soft teeth, with no hard enamel on the outside.

Urine contains chemicals that we use in cleaning fluids and used to be used for cleaning things.

There are 'banks' where the umbilical cords of new babies can be stored in case future medical developments make it possible to grow new organs or tissues from cells in them.

Scientists investigating tumour growth added a gene from a firefly to make a glow-in-the-dark tumour. The tumour is visible through the skin of a test animal, so scientists can see if it grows or shrinks.

Some animals respond to small amounts of poisonous gas and have been used as early warning systems. German soldiers kept cats in the trenches of the First World War to smell gas, and British miners kept budgies in cages because they died quickly if gas escaped into the mine.

A fear of worms is called *scoleciphobia*.

There are over 20,000 road crashes involving kangaroos in Australia every year, so a robo-roo robotic test crash dummy like a kangaroo is used to test how badly cars will be damaged.

A person would need to weigh around 650 kilograms (1,433 pounds) to have enough fat to stop a bullet. Although their body would be bullet-proof, they could still be killed by a shot to the head.

In 1999, an artist in Chicago, USA, announced his plan to grow a glow-in-the-dark dog by adding a gene from jellyfish to it.

Victorian children were often given their own salt cellar, which they were told was a sign of being grown up. In fact, the salt was mixed with *bromide*, which made them calmer and better behaved.

Police scientists investigating a murder can work out how long a body has been dead by looking at the kinds of maggots, worms and insects that are eating it.

Potatoes, aubergines, tomatoes and peppers all belong to the same family of plants as deadly nightshade!

Scientists are working on a microscopic robotic tadpole to deliver medicines – the tadpole would 'swim' through the patient's blood vessels to take the medicine where it's needed.

Not all dead bodies rot. In the right conditions, some of the fat can turn to a soap-like substance so that if the body is dug up, even years later, it can look much the same as when it was buried.

Archaeologists find out about what people in the Stone Age ate by examining Stone Age faeces called *coprolites*. They have to be soaked in water for three days first to soften them.

An unusual form of drug abuse is licking cane toads. They make a slime containing a drug which produces hallucinations (strange experiences or visions). People in some parts of Australia and the USA have started licking the toads to enjoy the drug.

Fake mermaids made from bits of monkey and fish have been produced to fool scientists for years – most recently with one claimed to have been washed up by the tsunami in Asia in 2004. The oldest so-called mummified mermaid is 1,400 years old and from Japan.

Australian Benjamin Drake Van Wissen invented machinery to mine guano on the Pacific island of Nauru and turn it into fertilizer.

Green potatoes contain a poison, *solanin*, which can be deadly. It develops in old potatoes that are not kept in the dark. Eating 2 kilograms (4.4 pounds) of green potatoes could be fatal.

If you are trapped in snow in an avalanche, it's impossible to tell which way is up (and so which way to dig yourself out). Urinate and see which direction the yellow stain spreads – gravity will pull the urine down.

Oil is made from the decayed bodies of animals and plants that died millions of years ago and have been squashed deep underground.

In 1822, Dr. William Beaumont studied human digestion as it happened, through a hole in the side and stomach of a patient who had been shot. The hole did not heal, allowing Dr. Beaumont to study, but also allowing food and drink to ooze out if it was not covered up.

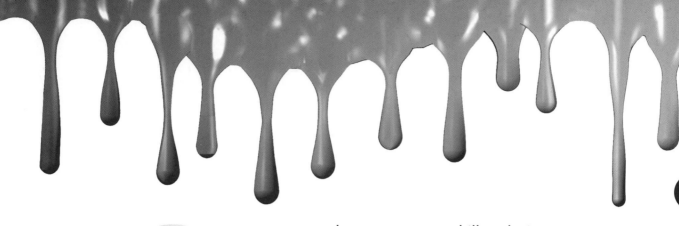

The most poisonous metal in the world is arsenic. It used to be made into fly papers for killing flies, but it killed some people, too.

In an attempt to kill malaria-carrying mosquitoes, an American scientist built towers to attract bats. He enticed them in with fabric covered with bat droppings, and played music near the bats' old homes to drive them out. After a few years, malaria infection dropped from 89 percent of the population to zero.

If you cut spinach with an iron knife, both will go black as a chemical in the spinach reacts with the iron.

During the First World War, goldfish were used to check whether all traces of poisonous gas had been washed out of gas masks. The mask was rinsed and filled with water, then a goldfish was dropped in. If it died, there was still gas left in it.

Around 1,400 years ago, the Chinese used to make gunpowder by boiling up and burning pig manure. To make sure it was ready, and not polluted with salt, they licked the crystals.

People used to use white lead powder to make their skin look white and beautiful, but it gave them lead poisoning and slowly killed them. As their skin looked worse once the poison took effect, they used more white lead to cover up the damage.

It can take a hundred years for the body of a whale at the bottom of the sea to disappear completely, as it is slowly eaten away by different animals, plants and microbes.

Early matches were made of poisonous chemicals and would sometimes burst into flames on their own if they got warm and damp. They poisoned the children employed to make them, and set fire to people's pockets unexpectedly!

Scraping mould off your food doesn't get rid of it – behind the fuzzy part you can see, strings extend into the food up to nine times the length of the visible part.

A small animal such as a mouse can be dropped 1,000 metres (3,280 feet) down a mineshaft and suffer no harm because the fastest speed it can fall it is not enough to crush its body. The larger an animal or object, the shorter the distance it can safely fall.

Our blood is red because it uses an iron compound to carry oxygen – some spiders have blue blood because theirs uses a copper compound instead.

John Haigh killed six people in London, UK, in the 1940s, dissolving their bodies in a bath of acid, hoping he could wash away all the evidence. However, on finding three human gallstones and a pair of dentures belonging to one of his victims in the sludge left behind, the police had enough evidence to convict him.

Old cannonballs brought up from the seabed can explode and kill divers. Bacteria eat away part of the metal, producing gases that rapidly expand when the cannonballs come to the surface.

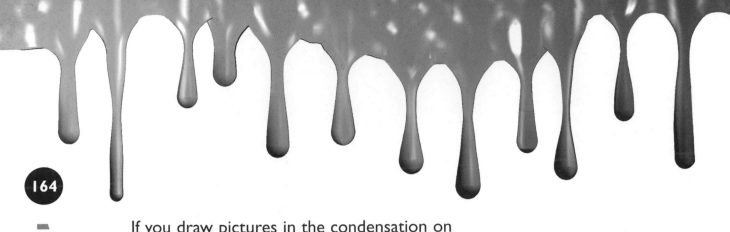

If you draw pictures in the condensation on a window, the picture will reappear next time the window mists over as a layer of grease from your skin stays on the glass and repels the water.

Earthworms bring 4 million kilograms (8.8 million pounds) of earth to the surface on every square kilometre (0.38 square miles) of open ground each year.

A medieval cure for stammering was scalding the tongue with a red-hot iron. It didn't work...

In the 1600s, spiders rolled in butter were recommended as a cure for malaria.

There have been several recorded cases of spontaneous human combustion (people who apparently burst into flames for no good reason). Sometimes, all that is left is a burnt patch and perhaps a foot or some singed clothing.

Rats trained to look for landmines are so light that they don't trigger the mechanism if they tread on one. Instead, they scratch and bite at the ground when they smell explosives, and the handler deals with the mine.

Horses killed in the First World War were recycled as explosives – their fat was removed and boiled down to be used in making TNT.

If you fall off a very high cliff or building, the fastest speed you will ever fall at is around 200 kilometres (124 miles) per hour. This is called terminal velocity, and it's enough to make a nasty splat.

Bird droppings are the main export of the island Nauru in the western Pacific Ocean. They're used for fertilizer, as they're rich in the chemical *nitrogen*.

Scientists believe that all *vertebrates* (animals with backbones) evolved from giant tadpoles, 6 centimetres (2.5 inches) long, that swam around 550 million years ago.

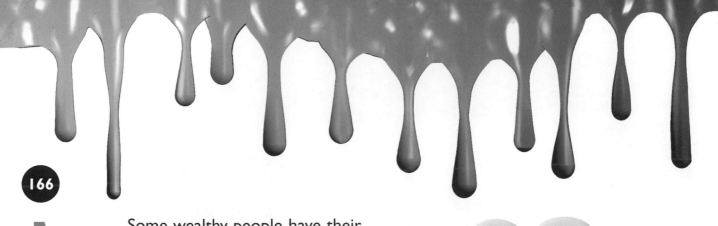

Some wealthy people have their bodies *cryopreserved* (deep-frozen) when they die, in the hope that in the future someone will find a cure for their cause of death and resurrect them. The popular urban legend that Walt Disney was cryopreserved is false; he was cremated.

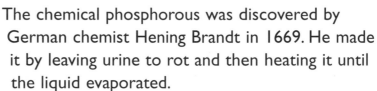

It is so cold in space, that urine flushed out of a space craft instantly freezes into a stream of yellow crystals.

If potatoes were discovered today, they would probably be banned under European Union regulations as too dangerous.

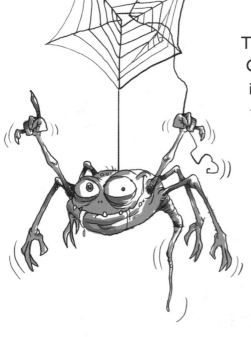

The chemical phosphorous was discovered by German chemist Hening Brandt in 1669. He made it by leaving urine to rot and then heating it until the liquid evaporated.

A man who experimented with feeding a Venus flytrap – a type of flesh-eating plant – with bits of his own flesh found the plant could digest it easily. He used bits of his toes that had rotted and dropped off as a result of athlete's foot.

Lined up neatly, 10,000 bacteria would stretch across your thumbnail.

There are 100 million times more insects than people on earth and their total weight is 12 times the total weight of people.

In an emergency, coconut milk can be used as substitute for the watery part of blood in a blood transfusion.

Japanese scientists have managed to grow tadpole eyes from scratch in the laboratory. They transplanted the eyes into tadpoles. The eyes worked even after the tadpoles changed into frogs.

The average bed is home to 6 million dust mites.

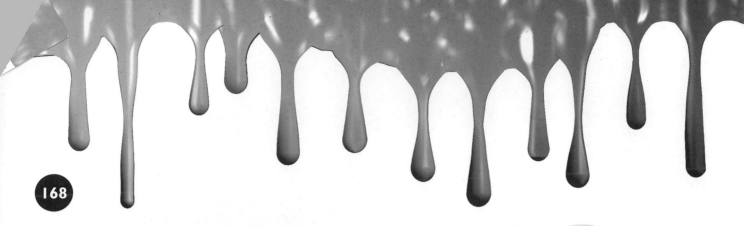

Ergot is fungus that grows on rye and causes people to act as though mad if they eat it. Some historians think that people accused of witchcraft who said they could fly, or those who accused others of strange, magical behaviour, may have had ergot poisoning.

The germs present in faeces can pass through 10 layers of toilet paper – that's why you need to wash your hands!

The largest living thing in the world is a fungus in Washington state, USA, which covers 6.5 square kilometres (2.5 square miles) and has been growing for hundreds of years.

The Masai tribe in Africa drink cow or bull urine as a sedative (drug to calm people down or make them sleepy).

There is a cockroach museum in Plano, Texas.

Some people – most of them in the USA – claim that they have been abducted by aliens from space while they slept, had their bodies experimented on and sometimes their minds changed, and were then returned to Earth.

It's said that dead Americans rot much more slowly than they used to – because they eat so many preservatives in their foods.

A will-o'-the-wisp is a flame of burning marsh gas that appears in boggy areas at night. It has lured many travellers to a muddy death when they have left the path to follow it, believing it to be someone with a light.

The castor bean plant contains the most deadly poison in the natural world, ricin. Just 70 micrograms (2-millionths of an ounce) could kill an adult human. It is 12,000 times more poisonous than rattle snake venom!

Bacteria – tiny living things that we also call germs – divide in two every 20 minutes. So, starting with one (it doesn't need a girlfriend/boyfriend), you can have over 130 million in just 9 hours!

Some scientists think that being too clean might make us ill – some studies suggest that people need to eat a small amount of dirt in order to kick start their immune systems. Not learning to fight infections can lead to asthma and other allergic problems.

The average glass of London tap water has passed through nine people's bladders before it reaches your sink.

One possible way of controlling cockroaches being explored in the USA is to release parasitic worms which will kill the roaches but don't harm people.

The stinking corpse plant, or *rafflesia*, is a huge parasitic flower that smells like rotting meat. The flower is up to a metre (about 3 feet) across and is the largest flower in the world. It grows directly out of a creeping vine, from which it gains all its nourishment without ever growing leaves of its own.

Scientists working on transplant techniques grew a human ear on the back of a mouse. The ear is moulded using human cartilage cells, and nourished by the mouse's blood as it grows.

Deodorants don't stop you sweating but they kill the bacteria that make sweat smell.

The earliest study of brain damage was of railway worker Phineas Gage. In 1848, an explosion shot a thick iron rod through his head. Although he recovered physically, his character changed completely. His skull and the iron rod are on display in Harvard University, USA.

A Roman cure for epilepsy (having fits) was to bathe in the blood of a gladiator.

A cure for whooping cough used in Yorkshire, England in the 1800s was to drink a bowl of soup with nine frogs hidden in it. You couldn't make it yourself – it only worked if you didn't know about the frogs. (And probably not then, either!)

Romans dressed small wounds with spider webs soaked in vinegar.

People on the Pacific island of Chuuk use a love potion made from centipede's teeth and stingray tails.

For centuries, it was illegal to cut up dead bodies, so surgeons and scientists had to pay criminals to steal the corpses of executed prisoners from the gallows in order to learn about anatomy.

An old cure for tuberculosis consisted of cutting open a newly dead cow, pulling the folds of skin around your neck and breathing in deeply.

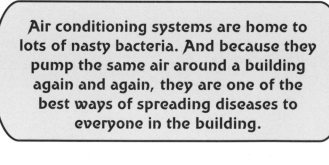

Air conditioning systems are home to lots of nasty bacteria. And because they pump the same air around a building again and again, they are one of the best ways of spreading diseases to everyone in the building.

A chemical extracted from leeches is used as a painkiller.

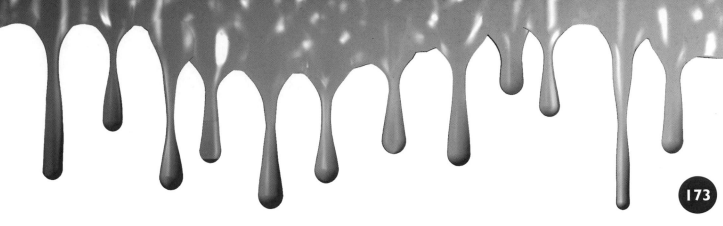

Electric bug zappers splatter an aerosol of dead bugs around the room as the bugs explode.

A medieval cure for meningitis involved splitting a pigeon in two and laying the two halves, cut side down, on the patient's head.

The Australian 1991 Inventor of the Year Award was won by the designer of a cockroach zapper. The roach is lured into a trap with food, then electrocuted.

If you flush the toilet without putting the seat down, a fine aerosol spray of urine and faeces flies into the air of the bathroom – and some lands on your toothbrush.

A stinging tree in Australia can cause intense pain and even death. Tiny hairs full of poison break off the leaves and stick to the skin, which can then heal over the injury, trapping the poison inside. Even standing near the tree can cause painful nosebleeds!

An old cure for a headache involved tying the rope used to hang a criminal around your temples.

A common cure for all kinds of illnesses in the past was 'bleeding' the patient. This could be done by the doctor making a small cut and putting a hot cup over the wound to suck out blood, or by putting blood-sucking leeches on the skin. Using leeches is being reintroduced by some western doctors.

In England in the 1500s, horse urine was rubbed into the scalp as a cure for baldness.

In the late 1800s, the Egyptian railways were fuelled by burning ancient mummies because they were more plentiful than coal and wood.

To catch the leeches for medical use, volunteers stand in rivers until the leeches attach themselves to their skin.

A treatment for the skin disease *psoriasis* available in Turkey involves sitting in a bath full of live fish, which eat away all the flaking skin.

The Venus flytrap is a plant with fleshy traps that look rather like a clam, edged with spikes. If an insect lands on the trap, the halves snap shut, trapping it, and then juices from the plant dissolve the insect for the plant to absorb.

Sometimes frozen blocks of toilet waste flushed from aeroplanes fall to earth.

To investigate what owls eat, scientists take apart owl pellets (owl faeces) and piece together the bones and fur from different creatures the owl has eaten.

One of the best ways of cleaning an infected wound, used before the days of antibiotics and now with infections that antibiotics can't treat, is to put maggots into it to eat the rotting flesh.

Sundew plants have lots of sticky tentacles. When an insect lands on them, it can't escape and the glue on the plant digests the insect's body, feeding the plant.

In 1986, 92 people were killed in Bangladesh by giant hailstones weighing up to 1 kilogram (2 pounds 3 ounces) each.

The English rhyme *Ring-a-Ring-o'-Roses* dates from the time of the bubonic plague. The 'roses' refer to red spots that appeared before boils started, the 'posies' to flowers people carried around to counteract the bad air that they thought caused plague, and the sneezing was an early symptom.

Scientists are working on a design for a spacecraft that will be partly fuelled by burning astronauts' faeces.

In the Middle Ages, people thought they could cure the medical condition *rheumatism* by carrying a dead shrew in their pockets.

The Fore people of Papua New Guinea traditionally eat the bodies of their dead relatives, including the brain. During the 1950s to 1960s an outbreak of the disease *kuru* was traced to the practice and people were dissuaded from enjoying the usual funeral meal.

The scientific name for fear of slime is *blennophobia*.

Some babies are born still enclosed in the sac that holds the fluid in which they develop in the womb. It used to be considered a sign of good luck. World War II leader Winston Churchill was born like this.

Taking a bath in the water used to wash a corpse was thought to cure epilepsy.

In the nineteenth century, arsenic was often used to create green colouring. A cake with green icing, coloured with arsenic, killed children who ate it at a birthday party, prompting chemists to ask for laws about what could be used in foods.

A new design for a rat trap sends a text message to a pest controller when it kills a rat, so that the rat can be quickly removed before it starts to decompose and smell.

Sometimes fish or frogs fall from the sky like rain – and there have been cases of a shower of meat (lumps of lung and muscle) and a rain of maggots.

Plants aren't as harmless as they seem. There are more than 600 types of carnivorous plants – plants that eat animals or insects.

Using genetic engineering techniques, scientists have a made a mouse that glows in the dark.

There are about 4,000 microbes above every 6.4 square centimetres (1 square inch) of ground.

Bodies buried in lead-lined coffins sometimes explode, as gases from the rotting body are held in by the strong metal. If they are dug up and opened, bits of body can fly out in all directions.

Equipment retrieved from the moon in the 1970s contained germs left there in 1967 – they were still alive.

The strangler fig grows from a seed dropped on another tree in bird or opossum faeces. It grows roots around the host tree and shades its leaves, eventually strangling the host tree to death.

Pitcher plants have a deep funnel filled with acid that dissolves any insects or small animals that fall into it. The dead creatures are used as food by the plant.

A zookeeper in Germany tried to treat an elephant for constipation with laxative foods and an enema (pumping oil into its anus through a tube). His cure was effective – the elephant produced 90 kilograms (200 pounds) of faeces, which landed on the keeper and suffocated him.

A firestorm is an uncontrollable fire, often the result of a bombing raid. Temperatures can rise to 800 degrees Celsius (1,472 degrees Fahrenheit) and air is sucked into the firestorm with the force of a hurricane. People who aren't burned can suffocate.

Fat contains a huge amount of energy. Polar explorers sometimes eat hunks of greasy seal fat to give themselves enough calories to keep their bodies warm.

Scabs are formed when chemical proteins react with special blood cells called platelets, which cause the blood to get sticky and clump together. Once you've clotted, lots of different chemicals and cells work together to dry out the clot and form a scab, keeping out germs while the cells underneath repair themselves. So, if you pick a scab you're messing with all your body's hard work!

A French cement factory uses soiled nappies as fuel to heat its cement kilns.

In 1890, a young girl was smeared with *phosphorous* so that she would glow in the dark and could act as a ghost in a hoax séance. She was poisoned by the chemical and died.

Piles of horse manure steam in cold weather because the action of bacteria breaking it down produces so much heat. The manure, filled with water and gas, is a good insulator, so it stays hot.

In 2000, UK mountaineer Major Michael Lane gave to a museum five of his own fingers and eight of his toes which had dropped off as a result of frostbite when he was climbing Mount Everest in 1976.

Volcanic vents deep under the sea are home to strange plants and animals that can live in high temperatures and poisonous, acidic water.

It is possible to drown in mud – and almost impossible to save someone who is drowning in mud as so much force is needed to pull them against the weight of it.

Scientists studying Mormon crickets cut the heads off to see what the crickets had been eating – and found many had eaten other Mormon crickets. If one stopped to eat, another would often come along and eat it.

Doctors used to test for diabetes by tasting the patient's urine – diabetes made it taste sweet because sugar was lost in it.

The first frozen chicken was created by Sir Francis Bacon who stuffed a plucked chicken with snow in 1626 to experiment with refrigeration. It worked, but he died from a chill contracted during the experiment. The chicken is said to haunt Pond Square in London.

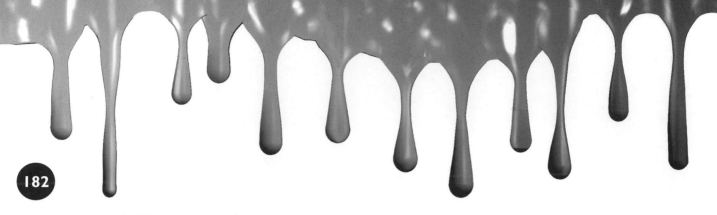

If blue whales tried to live on land, they would be crushed and suffocated by their own weight. They can live successfully in water because it supports them.

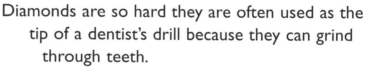

In an experiment with a condemned prisoner, Doctor Beaurieux of France discovered in 1905 that a person – or head – can hear and respond for around 25 seconds after beheading.

Diamonds are so hard they are often used as the tip of a dentist's drill because they can grind through teeth.

On the east coast of the USA there is a laboratory that leaves dead bodies of humans and animals outside to decay so that scientists can study the rate at which they rot, and the maggots and microbes that help them decompose.

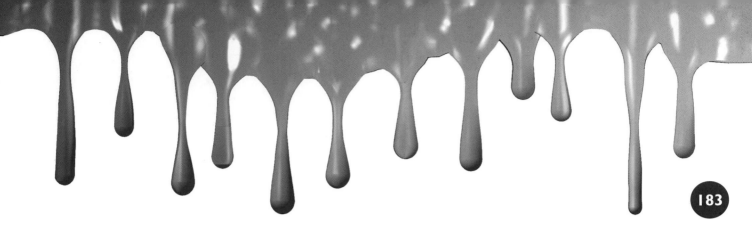

Hungry huskies and polar bears have been known to attack explorers when they urinate – they are attracted by the smell.

Honey kills germs. Spreading it on wounds can stop them becoming infected.

> Scientists have modified cockroaches, implanting electrodes in them to control their legs, and used them as living robots to carry cameras or explosives through tiny spaces.

Soap can be made by dissolving animal fat using an alkali such as *sodium hydroxide*. Soap used to be made from sheep or pig fat.

Most bacteria are only about 0.00025 of a centimetre (0.0001 of an inch) across. But monster bacteria have been found at the bottom of the ocean off the coast of Africa. They are so big they can be seen without a microscope – they're each about the size of the dot of this full stop.

Dermestid beetles are so good at stripping the flesh off dead animals that natural history museums use their larvae to clean up skeletons they are going to put on display.

Some types of pitcher plant have long trailing stems which capture and digest small animals such as frogs.

Amongst fuels investigated for use where (or when) oil and petrol are scarce, scientists have tried running cars and tractors on chicken faeces.

Occasionally, babies are born with a full set of teeth.

In Chile, trains on the Arica-La Paz railway were at one time powered by burning llama faeces.

Horrible World Record Facts

CAUTION!: Some of these World Record Facts involve dangerous activities. They have been set by people who have had proper medical guidance. Don't try any of them at home!

Charles Osbourne, from Iowa, USA, hiccupped every 1.5 seconds for 69 years and then suddenly stopped.

The most expensive coffee in the world is made with coffee beans recovered from the faeces of the civet, a type of wild cat from Sumatra.

At a single meal, obese New Yorker Walter Hudson could eat:
12 doughnuts, 10 packets of crisps,
8 Chinese take-aways and half a cake!

Peter Dowdeswell of the UK ate a three-course meal in a record 45 seconds in 1999. He ate oxtail soup, mashed potatoes, baked beans and sausage, and then prunes.

Natasha Verushka of the USA holds the record for sword-swallowing; she swallowed 13 swords at a convention in 2004.

The biggest cockroach in the world is the Madagascan hissing cockroach. It can grow to 9 centimetres (3.5 inches) – as long as an adult's finger.

Monte Pierce of the USA can flick a coin 3.3 metres (10 feet 10 inches) with his earlobes.

The black-headed sea snake found north of Australia in the Timor Sea is 100 times more deadly than the most poisonous snake on land.

Leonardo d'Andrea from Italy smashed 32 watermelons with his head in 1 minute in 2005.

Kevin Cole from the USA shot a strand of spaghetti out of his nose a distance of 19 centimetres (7.5 inches) in 1998.

Marc Quinquandon, from France, set a world record by eating 144 snails in 11 minutes. He beat his own record when he ate 72 snails in 3 minutes, but he died soon afterwards.

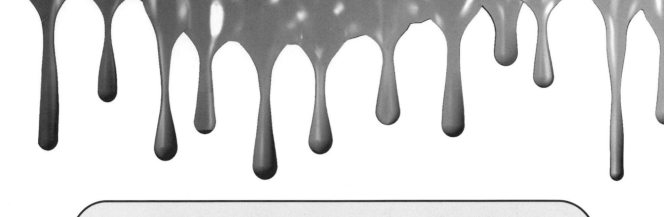

In 2005, Matthew Henshaw from Australia swallowed a sword 40.5 centimetres (15.9 inches) long, and hung a sack of potatoes weighing 20 kilograms (44 pounds 5 ounces) on its handle for 5 seconds.

The biggest beetle in the world is the dung-eating Goliath beetle – it's about the size of a hamster!

In 1998, 13 year-old Daniel Canal of Miami, USA, received 12 transplanted organs in only 3 weeks.

The loudest recorded scream was 129 decibels, made by Jill Drake of the UK at a Halloween celebration in 2000.

By March 2005, American Donald Gorske had eaten 20,500 Big Macs. He has eaten at least one a day for 33 years.

Gordon Cates of the USA holds the record for kissing poisonous snakes. He kissed 11 cobras in 1999.

A woman who worked on smelly feet in a testing laboratory had to smell 5,600 feet over 15 years.

A Japanese woman holds the record for having most worms removed from her stomach; doctors removed a total of 56 in 1990.

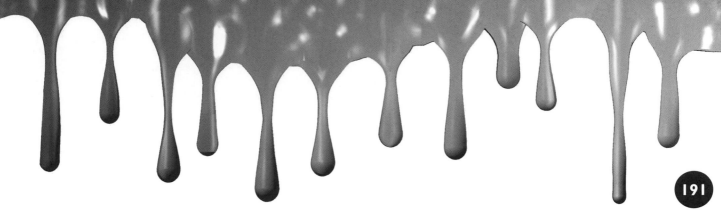

Tom Shufflebottham charmed 511 worms out of the ground at a worm-charming championship in England in 1980.

Norman Gary of the USA held 109 live honey bees in his mouth for 10 seconds in 1998.

In 1997, an Egyptian boy of 16 was found to have his unborn identical twin growing inside him. It had died at about 32–33 weeks old and was 45 centimetres (18 inches) long.

Danny Capps holds the record for spitting a dead cricket out of his mouth, reaching a distance of 9.17 metres (30 feet).

Michael Lloyd of the USA holds the record for kicking himself in the head – 42 times in a row!

Hu Saelao of Thailand has not cut his hair for more than 70 years.

The two smelliest substances are gross gases which the US government is investigating as possible weapons. They would be used to break up crowds without harming people. One is called 'Who Me?' and the other 'The US Government Standard Bathroom Malodor'.

Ken Edwards of the UK ate 36 live cockroaches in one minute on a breakfast TV show in 2001.

Ciro Gallo of the UK holds the record for having concrete blocks broken on his chest with a sledge hammer, while lying on a bed of nails – 37 blocks weighing a total of 235.8 kilograms (519.8 pounds).

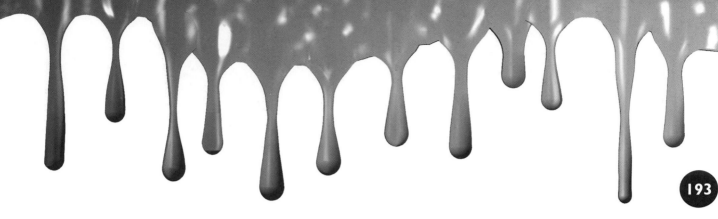

In 1999, American Scott Jeckel shot a marshmallow 4.96 metres (16.27 feet) out of his nose, with his friend Ray Perisin catching it in his mouth.

The longest-lasting operation took 96 hours and was carried out in Chicago, USA, in 1951 to remove a giant tumour.

Dustin Phillips of the USA can drink a whole bottle of tomato ketchup through a straw in only 33 seconds.

Shridhar Chillal grew his fingernails for 44 years without cutting them. Their average length was 117 centimetres (46 inches), and his thumbnail was 132 centimetres (52 inches).

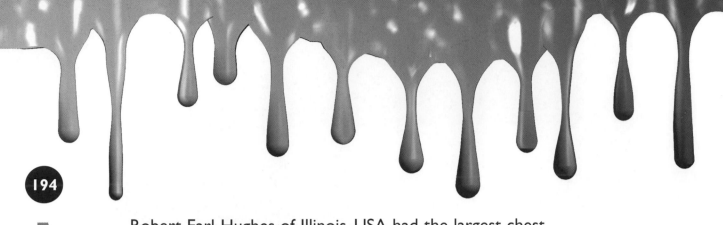

Robert Earl Hughes of Illinois, USA had the largest chest measurement ever recorded. He was 3.15 metres (10 feet 4 inches) around the chest when he died, aged 32. He weighed 484 kilograms (1,067 pounds).

In 1976, American Jon Brower Minoch weighed 635 kilograms (1,400 pounds). He was so fat that it took 12 firemen to lift him out of his house when he fell ill, and 13 nurses to turn him over in bed. In fact, he had two beds strapped together as one wasn't big enough to hold him. He once put on 89 kilograms (196 pounds) in a single week.

The smallest fully-grown adult ever to live was Gul Mohammed of India, who was 57 centimetres (34.5 inches) tall at the age of 33 and weighed only 17 kilograms (37.5 pounds).

The record for spitting a mouthful of tobacco is 16.23 metres (53 feet 3 inches), set in 1997.

The longest recorded eyebrow hair was 7.8 centimetres (3.1 inches) long.

The worst epidemic of all time was the Black Death – a plague carried by fleas that live on rats – which killed 75 million people in Europe and Asia between 1347 and 1351.

The most poisonous fish in the world is the stone fish. Treading on its spines causes a painful death in 20 minutes.

A hairball weighing 2.53 kilograms (5 pounds 3 ounces) was removed from the stomach of a 20 year-old English woman in 1895.

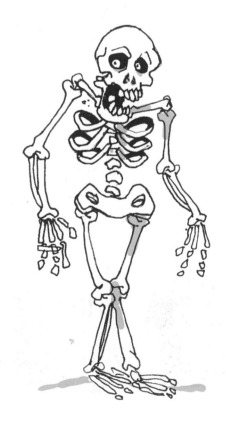

The largest ever kidney stone – a solid mass of mineral that collects inside the kidneys – weighed 356 grams (12.5 ounces). It was removed from a man in Australia in 2003.

The longest leg hair grew on Australian man Tim Stinton – it was 12.4 centimetres (4.9 inches) long.

The winner of a fly-swatting contest in 1912 killed 543,360 flies, weighing a total of 96 kilograms (212 pounds).

Kim Goodman from the USA can 'pop' her eyeballs out of their sockets so that they stick out 11 millimetres (0.4 inches).

Motorcycle stunt rider Evel Knievel of Montana, USA, holds the record for broken bones – he suffered 435 fractures while working as stunt rider.

A man in Bulgaria who accidentally shot himself in 1942 still has the bullet lodged in his head.

Thomas Wedders, who lived in England in the 1770s, is said to have had a nose 19 centimetres (7.5 inches) long.

The youngest person to have a full set of false teeth was only 4 years old. He suffered from an inherited disease that destroyed his teeth.

American Robert Wadlow had the largest feet ever recorded. They were 47 centimetres (18.5 inches) long.

Garry Turner of the UK can stretch a flap of skin away from his body to a length of 15.8 centimetres (6.25 inches). He has a medical condition that affects his skin making it super-elastic.

Monte Pierce from the USA can stretch his left ear lobe to a length of 12.7 centimetres (5 inches).

Stephen Taylor from the UK can stick his tongue out 9.4 centimetres (3.7 inches) measured from the tip to his lips.

The longest beard ever was grown by Hans Langseth of Norway, whose whiskers stretched an incredible 5.33 metres (17.6 inches) when measured on his death in Kensett, Iowa, in 1927. The beard was presented to the Smithsonian Institution, Washington DC, in 1967.

Giovanni Batista from Orsenigo, Italy, has a collection of more than 2 million human teeth.

Shamsher Singh from India has the longest beard on a living man. In 1997, it was 1.83 metres (6 feet) long.

Thomas Blackthorne of the UK can lift 11 kilograms (24 pounds) of weights using just his tongue.

Rene Alvarenga of El Salvador has eaten 35,000 live scorpions. He catches them himself with his bare hands and eats 20 to 30 per day.

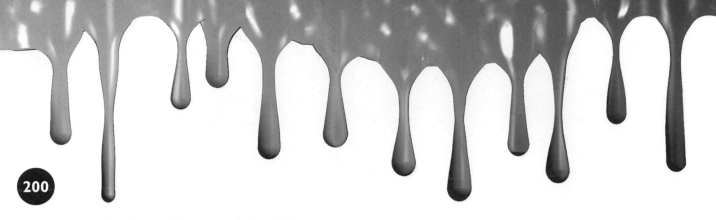

Garry Turner of the UK once clipped 159 wooden clothes pegs to his face at the same time.

French man Michel Lotito is called Monsieur Mangetout (Mr. Eat Everything) because since 1959 he has been snacking on all kinds of glass and metal. He's eaten a computer, 18 bicycles, an aeroplane, 6 chandeliers, 15 supermarket trolleys, 2 beds, 7 TV sets and a pair of skis. In total, he's eaten more than 9 tonnes (1,984 pounds) of metal.

Letchemanah Ramasamy from Malaysia has pulled a double-decker bus 30 metres (around 98 feet), using only his hair.

Wim Hof of the Netherlands exposed his whole body to ice for 1 hour 8 minutes using yoga and meditation to stop himself freezing.

Meng Xu of China can thread 20 needles in his mouth using just his tongue. He did it in 6 minutes and 45 seconds in 2003.

Two people from the USA share the record for sitting in a bathtub with 75 live rattlesnakes.

The largest recorded snail was an Africa giant snail 39.3 centimetres (15.5 inches) long.

The largest tumour removed in one piece from a living person weighed 137.6 kilograms (303 pounds) and was 1 metre (3 feet across). It weighed more than the woman it was growing inside.

The loudest recorded burp was produced by Paul Hunn of the UK in 2004. It measured nearly 105 decibels – as loud as a fast underground train whizzing past!

The largest snail ever found was 39.3 centimetres (15.5 inches) long and weighed 900 grams (2 pounds).

The largest rubbish tip in the world is Fresh Kills landfill, New York, USA. It is thought to contain 100 million tonnes (98 million tons) of rubbish and covers 1,200 hectares (3,000 acres).

Zafar Gill of Pakistan can lift 51.7 kilograms (113 pounds 15 ounces) of weights with a clamp attached to his right ear.

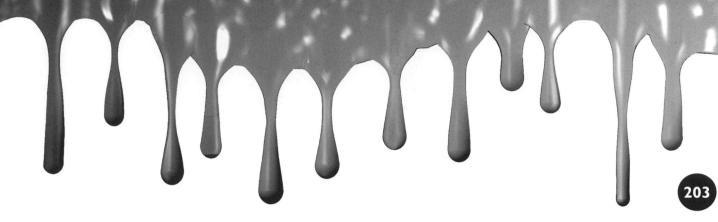

American Gary Bashaw can mix chocolate powder and milk in his mouth and pour it out of his nose as milkshake. In 1999, he made a record-breaking 54 millilitres (1.8 ounces) of milkshake in one go.

Over a period of 40 years, American Charles Jensen had 970 operations to remove tumours (lumps), mostly from his face.

A bootlace worm washed up on the shore of Scotland in 1864 was 55 metres (180 feet) long.

Clint Hallam from New Zealand has lost the same hand (the right one) three times – in 1984 it was cut off in an accident and doctors re-attached it; it was removed again in 1989 when it got infected; a new, transplanted hand was removed in 2001 after rejection problems.

A man known as Snake Manu, from India, swallowed 200 earthworms each at least 10 centimetres (4 inches) long in 30 seconds in 2003.

Tom Leppard from the UK has his whole body tattooed with leopard spots, the spaces between being tattooed yellow. This makes him the most tattooed person in the world.

In 1999, Brad Byers of the USA swallowed 10 swords each 68.5 centimetres (27 inches) long, and rotated them through 180 degrees in his throat.

The worst flu epidemic ever came in 1918 at the end of World War I. It killed 21 million people – twice as many as died in the war.

Marco Hort of Switzerland can fit 258 drinking straws in his mouth at the same time.

The fattest man in the world, Walter Hudson of New York, USA, had a waist measurement of more than 3 metres (9 feet 11 inches).

Kama Muk of the UK bravely had 600 new body piercings in a single day in 2002.

A British woman has 2,520 body piercings including a hole in her tongue large enough to poke a finger through.

The heaviest living snake is a Burmese Python that weighs nearly 183 kilograms (403 pounds) and is 71 centimetres (28 inches) round. It lives in a safari park in the USA.

The fastest eater is the star-nosed mole. It can identify something as edible, catch and eat it in 120 milliseconds.

The largest jellyfish was 2.28 metres (7 feet 6 inches) across the body and had a tentacle-span of 36.5 metres (120 feet).

At the largest frogs' legs eating festival ever, in Florida, 2001, 13,200 people ate 3,000 kilograms (6,600 pounds) of frogs' legs fried in batter.

The longest recorded snake was a python 10 metres (35 feet 9.5 inches) long.

> The most poisonous animal in the world is probably the two-toned arrow-poison frog – only 28 grams (1 ounce) of its poison could kill nearly 3 million people.

Nick Thompson of the UK holds the record for eating baked beans with a cocktail stick – he ate 136 in 3 minutes.

> During heart surgery in 1970, a patient with *haemophilia* (an inherited condition which stops the blood clotting) needed 1,080 litres of blood – nearly 15 baths full – as he kept bleeding.

Dean Gould of England can pick 50 winkles (a shellfish like a small snail) from shells with a pin in 1 minute 22 seconds.

Your 1001st Horrible Fact !

I, the reader, hereby confirm that this is the grossest fact I know.

Signed: ....

Date: ....